T0375535

PRAYER PAVES THE WAY

INSPIRING REFLECTIONS
ON LIVING WITH THE
HOLY SPIRIT

MARILYN BODINE
WITH PATRICIA LEACH

WESTBOW
PRESS®
A DIVISION OF THOMAS NELSON
& ZONDERVAN

WestBow Press books may be ordered through booksellers or by contacting:

WestBow Press
A Division of Thomas Nelson & Zondervan
1663 Liberty Drive
Bloomington, IN 47403
www.westbowpress.com
844-714-3454

ISBN: 979-8-3850-1693-8 (sc)
ISBN: 979-8-3850-1694-5 (hc)
ISBN: 979-8-3850-1693-8 (e)

Library of Congress Control Number: 2024901064

Print information available on the last page.

WestBow Press rev. date: 03/21/2024

To Jesus and the Holy Spirit, whose entry into
my life opened my heart, mind, and spirit to a
new world filled with hope, joy, and love.

Life took on new meaning, so rich and wonderful that I
welcome everyone to share in this marvelous experience of
love. This love never diminished or disappeared in my life.

CONTENTS

FOREWORD

The Great Commission

If you have decided to read this book, you are about to embark on a magnificent journey. This book is filled with real-time stories that reflect the life and learnings of Marilyn Bodine, my friend and spiritual mentor. This journey, however, is for you! Hang on; this book has the potential to change the way you think about your life! Throughout these pages, you will read stories of how the Holy Spirit manifested in people's lives in transformational and astonishing ways. You will learn how Marilyn's surrender to God opened glorious doors to the kingdom.

Here is what you may find surprising and simultaneously very exciting, should you accept this challenge. You are invited to use this book as your personal workbook. Consider for a moment that the thrilling stories contained within can be yours. Our God is still in the business of miracles. As a child of God, you have the right to claim your authority, and with this authority, the gates of the kingdom open because God is calling all His children to participate in a wondrous, faith-filled, miracle-producing walk.

When I first met Marilyn Bodine and her co-teacher Franny Clark, there was a great deal that I did not understand. I was what some call a *cradle Catholic*. I believed that all authority rested wholly with the leaders of the church. It was what I was taught, and I had no reason to believe otherwise. I attended church and truly sought to know God more intimately. I didn't see myself as having much of a role to play, at least not in the larger scheme of things, and certainly not in praying for the sick or expecting miracles. I wasn't a priest or a church leader; that was their job.

The classes offered by Marilyn and Franny, whom you will come to meet in this book, changed my life. The many students came from all walks of life and various church denominations. But that didn't matter. Every story and every teaching presented to the eager pupils was centered on Jesus. It was the heart of every lesson. Jesus said, "I am the way, the truth, and the life" (John 14:6 NVS). Christ invites us to go into the world and make disciples of nations (Matthew 28:16–20). God has given His people a huge assignment. First, however, I had to learn how.

During this training period of my life, I began to see that I had many roles—a wife, a mother, a teacher, a friend, and a church layperson—but my roles represented what I did, not who I was. I began to realize an astounding truth. My identity is as a child of God, and that identity comes with powerful authority. This was when I began to understand my true life's purpose. It was the very commission that God set out for me as referenced in Jeremiah 1:5 (KJV), "Before I formed you in the womb, I knew you, before you were born, I set you apart; I appointed you as a prophet to the nations." Once I understood this responsibility and opportunity, I fully embraced it. Once I accepted it, my life took on a fullness I had never known before.

Marilyn showed me that we all have unique spiritual gifts through love and Christian patience. She would remind us of Paul's words in 1 Corinthians 12:12 (NIV), "Just as a body, though one, has many parts, but all its many parts for one body, so it is with Christ." What matters is that we accept our identity in

Christ and all things are possible through Him. We need one another, and by needing one another and serving together, we enhance each other's unique gifts. My sincere hope is that as you read about Marilyn's life work, history, and journey with the Father, Son, and Holy Spirit, you will discover yourself. We are all being commissioned.

I will repeat Jesus's words in the book of Matthew:

> Then the eleven disciples went to Galilee, to the mountain where Jesus had told them to go. When they saw him, they worshipped him, but some doubted. Then Jesus came to them and said, "All authority in heaven and on earth has been given to me. Therefore, go and make disciples of all nations, baptizing them in the name of the Father and of the Son and of the Holy Spirit, and teaching them to obey everything I have commanded you. And surely I am with you always, to the very end of the age." (Matthew 28:16–20 NIV)

May the words in this book bless your life forever.

Maria Spina
A student and friend of Marilyn Bodine

ACKNOWLEDGMENTS

There are so many people to thank and appreciate who have accompanied me on my journey.

To the Clark family, particularly Franny and Mary Beth, who became my spiritual family as we walked together on the journey with Jesus, helping one another to always take the next step.

To my wonderfully gifted and deeply loving family, who never gave up on me through troubled times and with whom the Lord provided the love to bring healing to all of us.

To my many wonderful friends who opened their hearts to help me grow spiritually with Jesus even when it seemed like I was standing still or unsure if I was really hearing the Holy Spirit speak. I thank you for your never-ending patience, generosity, and love. I am so grateful to all of you.

My deepest gratitude to the special friends who continually nudged me to "write a book" because the Lord had put in their hearts to encourage me to do so. Thank you for continuing to push me about it even when I sometimes didn't want to hear it.

In particular, thank you, Patricia Leach, who listened to God's nudging to help me put my words into a story format. Thank you for writing the stories I shared with the gift from the Holy Spirit. It is one thing to be able to tell a story but quite another to modify, change, research the information, and then sit down and allow the Holy Spirit to clean it up. This was always followed by fruitful working sessions with Diane Glover, who used her remarkable skills to ensure that clarity existed throughout the pages.

Thank you to all the faith-filled friends who have accompanied me on this wonderful journey.

INTRODUCTION

The year I began this book was a significant year for me. It was the year of my ninetieth birthday.

I am grateful for the many birthdays God has blessed me with, and as I reflect on my abundant years of life, it is now with a deeper and more meaningful understanding of how God guided me through many challenges. Some of my trials were real while others were the consequences of my personal struggle caused by a refusal to accept anything that didn't suit my mental purview of what my life should be. I grew up in the Midwest as part of a large, rambunctious family that enjoyed life and one another. We embodied the Midwestern values of that era. My early recollections are filled with memories of generous family affection. This comfortable and gracious environment made me ill-prepared for the onslaught that faced me in my early teens—succumbing to the epidemic of polio that left my body weak with exhaustion. Also, my parents' divorce occurred at a time when the breakup of a family created community chatter and what I perceived as unwanted stares.

With the benefit of twenty-twenty hindsight, I can now see that in my darkest and most challenging moments, God was always present, and often His presence came in the way of a person or a group of people. In like-minded communities, I found God's presence flourishing among His people who chose to walk together.

He brought my dearest friend Frances Clark to me exactly when I needed a stable and soothing voice to calm my fears and frustrations. Frances was the start of "my" community. Together, we shared many moving experiences on our journey to a closer relationship with God. I reflect on our extraordinary voyage to the Holy Land in this book. The return home from this trip was a pivotal moment in my life because it was then that I began to understand the importance of community and having fellow voyagers on our spiritual journey.

In preparation for writing this book, I found something I had written almost fifty years ago that reflected on community and the immeasurable experiences we shared. Now with the wisdom of these many decades, which through my rearview mirror gives me much more clarity, I can attest that what we were all thinking and feeling way back then still holds true today. Here is what I wrote,

> Where are we going? In these critical times, it is important to understand how to grow in God's grace to combat a very active enemy who is attempting to tear down the Kingdom of God.

As I began reviewing my life's journey for the purposes of this book, I wasn't sure where it would take me. As the days, weeks, and months evolved, and I revisited my long-ago experiences, I had an *aha* moment of gigantic proportions.

As depicted in this book, my journey would not have been possible without becoming acquainted with the Holy Spirit, the third and oftentimes unknown person of the Trinity. He is our guide, comforter, spokesperson, and everything we could ever want or need. As a child, I prayed to Jesus. I knew He was present although my conversations with Him would sometimes ebb and flow. I always knew, however, that if I were in trouble, I could—and frantically did—call upon Jesus for His help.

As I reflect, I now appreciate that after I met the Holy Spirit, an experience detailed in this book, everything changed. I met a star-quality intercessor. I recall driving frantically through congested highways, worried that I would be late for a conference speech, and then after asking for the intercession of the Holy Spirit, the roads would clear. I was always on time!

Children who learn about Christ's love early in life are usually taught to pray to Jesus. If we could teach children and for that matter, all adults the easy availability of the Holy Spirit, it would change the world.

As you read this book, I pray that you will be filled with the power of the Holy Spirit and come to know Christ more profoundly through the third person in the Trinity.

In fact, I am claiming Paul's words in Ephesians 1:17–19 (NIV) for every reader, "I keep asking that the God of our Lord Jesus Christ, the glorious Father, may give you the Spirit of wisdom and revelation so that you may know him better. I pray that the eyes of your heart may be enlightened so that you may know the hope to which he has called you, the riches of his glorious inheritance in his holy people, and his incomparably great power for us who believe."

As we walk together, awaiting the beautifully set banquet table that has been prepared for us, God desires for us during our preparation to have community; the Lord desires for us to have healthy families; the Lord desires us to have holy friendships; and with the mighty intercessions of Holy Spirit, we are able to live out the desires of our Heavenly Father.

If you have not done so, consider inviting the Holy Spirit into your life.

1

FACING THE MUSIC AND THIS ISN'T DANCING

I LOOKED ACROSS THE length of the passenger railway dining car, and with the sounds of clattering dishes in the background, I was momentarily stunned. I was bewildered and simultaneously certain that the face I was staring at, which was also staring back at me, was the woman I called mother. Why would she be on this train? I pondered on many reasons but found none.

Was my life of lies, deception, and fleeing as quickly as I could away from God about to be exposed right now? Had I gotten to the end of my string of lies?

The year was 1955. I had fled my chaotic home in St. Louis more than two years before and enrolled at Missouri State University in Columbia. Angry with the world, I skipped courses, wasted hours upon hours, and made it a point to let everyone know that I didn't like the people, didn't enjoy the classes, and was living life on my own terms: carefree and unconcerned!

The truth is, attending the state university in Columbia, Missouri, was not my first escape.

Two years before, my mother had given me an ultimatum.

I was embarrassed and angry because I had been stricken with polio at the tender age of fourteen during the peak of its outbreak, and I was emotionally broken by my parent's divorce, which proved fodder for the local newspaper. I didn't have the words to justify or the courage to express my feelings, but I certainly had actions that unquestionably conveyed my emotions. Quite literally, I was impossible to live with. Rules were not my thing.

Much like my father, I was a great storyteller. My only challenge was that my infinite imagination often did not resemble truth. My mother delivered the final blow when she said, "If you don't want to be part of this family, you can go."

Wait. What? Go? Where would I go?

As a child of divorce, I had an option. I went to live with my father and his new wife. That would teach my mother how determined her daughter was! That lasted for about a year, and to everyone's great relief, they said goodbye as I headed to Columbia, Missouri, to become a freshman at the state university. I wanted out of town and I thought I wanted out of my family, and they were more than happy to oblige.

Now more than two years later, without much to show for my time at the state university and knowing that I was not going to be invited to return the following year, I made up a new lie. Visiting my family on a short break, I announced that I had been accepted at Stanford University in California. Yes, I was Stanford bound!

It was at this time my mother received a call that my brother Bob, who lived in Salt Lake City, had been injured in an accident. My mother was asked to help care for him during his recovery.

A plan was set. My mother and I would drive west in what was called a drive-away car in those days. I would drop her off at Salt Lake City and proceed to Stanford University. It was expected that I would return the car and begin my new life at this prestigious university.

Shortly after I arrived in California, I returned the car, and then abruptly and without warning, all my lies, misdeeds, and baseless actions came to a roaring head. Here I am. What am I going to do? I didn't have a job. I didn't have money. I certainly hadn't been accepted at Stanford, and in approximately one week, I would be homeless. The cold, hard reality of the life I had created was beginning to set in. I was scared and very alone.

For the first time in my young life, I was confronted by the consequences of my actions, and I knew I had to face the music. I was forced to return home and had to face the truth. With any luck, my mother wouldn't return home for weeks.

Boarding a return railcar, the first night was spent playing cards and drinking beers with a group of American soldiers returning from active duty. After all, there was a little time to drown in the looming reality before I had to face the music. The next morning, after a night of hilarious laughter and fun, I slipped into the dining car for breakfast. It was then that I saw her! Immediately, I choked, and despite having nothing to eat, there was a lump in my throat that was too big to swallow. I panicked. My mom was sitting before me.

My mother looked up, and without displaying any visible facial reaction, she beckoned me. She said in a low voice, her face close to mine, "What are you doing here?"

As I stood before my mother on the speeding train that day, I knew there was no going back. A brief review of my life brought me up short. My relationship with my mother was complicated. She spoke with great authority, and I loved her, yet I behaved in ways that were completely opposite to how I felt. My mother could scare the daylights out of me, yet I would push the envelope to deliberately infuriate her.

For instance, I knew my mother hated lies, yet I took vicarious pleasure in lying. As an adult, I reflected on those moments when lying became part of my subconscious behavior. On one occasion, when I was around three years old, I was dancing around the room in a circle. I was so joy-filled that all the attention was focused on me as I exuberantly shared a story. My Aunt Dorothy looked at me and broadly proclaimed to everyone in the room, "Marilyn, you shoot the bull too much!" I quickly responded, "Me shoot one bull, me shoot two bulls, me shoot all the bulls." Everyone laughed at my little-girl antics, but at that moment, I knew it was my job to make sure my storytelling entertained the audience. After that, when the family would see me coming, they would say, "Here comes the bull shooter." I now had a reputation to uphold.

Unwittingly what began as an entertaining story ended up becoming something that damaged my emotional development. It also had another effect. I was labeled a liar. I was often charged with picking up my little sister Grace from school. Later in the evening, Grace would delight in reporting to my mother that I would speed as much as seventy-seven miles per hour on the highway. Even though I would say it wasn't true, my mother would always respond, "Don't lie to me. Your sister tells the truth, and I had better not catch you speeding."

One might wonder how I could look back on those years without embarrassment or even write about them, but it is at this moment of truth, standing in that railroad car, that I look back and realize God was beckoning me. This wasn't the first time, but it was the first time that I was listening.

This is my story about God's miraculous love.

By the time I reached adolescence, anger had been my go-to coping mechanism. If I didn't get my way or something didn't go precisely as planned, my wrath would erupt, and I'd be able to inflict pain with my practiced tongue.

Much of my rage stemmed from the many years of uncertainty while I recovered from polio. Up until the feared disease polio entered our lives, my childhood was filled with wonderful family antics and joyous laughter. The war had ended, and my family was enjoying great prosperity. I was able to freely partake in my favorite summer activity—swimming!

My mother had arranged a summer vacation for my sister and me at a resort on one of Wisconsin's many lakes. Each day I would enjoy the feeling of the water surrounding my body as I bopped up and down the lakes and various swimming holes. I would swim until I was quite literally exhausted from play.

A few days after I returned home from our summer outing, I awoke from a long night's sleep and attempted to get out of bed. I immediately fell to the ground. What happened? I slowly pulled myself back to bed, rested, and got up again. This time I crashed weightily on the floor with a loud thud. This instantly brought my mother and father to my side. I could see the anxiousness on their faces as they helped me back to bed.

A quick consult between my parents resulted in a call to the family doctor. In those days, doctors made house calls, and it didn't take too long for him to arrive at our home. After a quick physical examination and a subsequent visit to a specialist, it was confirmed that I had fallen victim to the epidemic sweeping the country: the dreaded disease called polio.

The treatments at that time were limited, but with my mother's determination to search for any remedies available, I began a relentless routine of hot packs and other therapies. By the spring of the following year, I was sent to a polio ward where I would slowly learn to walk again.

Looking back, I realized that during the many years of recovering from polio, I was forced to give up many things I loved doing, and by virtue of that loss, I had also lost personal control. Swimming, badminton, and the many youthful activities that were regularly part of my life would never exist for me again. When my legs gave out beneath me, my heart was silently heavy with the question, *Will I ever walk again?* In my adolescent way, anger gave me back some measure of control. It fueled me and kept me afloat.

Being a member of a family whose DNA expected achievement, my anger defined me. My parents' subsequent divorce turned anger into rage. Their settlement ensured that I would receive one hundred dollars a month for my care. I was insistent that the money should be given directly to me, and I was fuming when it wasn't. It was my money! When my dad offered me a brand-new Bulova wristwatch on the condition that I walked in thirty days, I ensured that he would have to make good on that promise! Stuck in my lonely room for months on end, I dwelled on the hand that had been dealt me.

My wrath reached its apex one day. It was a moment of such defiance that I knew I had to find a way to hide my emotions. My mother, who was doing her best to be a loving mother despite her hurt from the divorce and the challenge of an invalid daughter, was calling me to account for my unmanageable behaviors. I remember vividly sitting on the porch with her when I took offense to what she was saying. I picked up a hammer within my reach, and I mentally imagined myself hitting her. It took every ounce of strength I had not to bludgeon her with the hammer I was holding. I believe that God stayed my hand that day, but I took my fury inward at that moment. My behavior shocked even me, but I didn't have anyone to help me understand that unless I learned how to deal with my emotions, they would continue to dictate my irrational behavior. Like a castaway treasure, I buried my anger deep within my soul. It remained within me, now hidden, but it was ready to spring to life given the right circumstances.

Eventually, I returned to school although I looked much different, and I was now a year behind my classmates. Walking required the assistance of two *Kenny sticks*. These sticks had been developed by Sr. Elizabeth Kenny, an Australian nurse who had pioneered polio treatments as early as 1910. These sticks helped me walk, but they were positioned halfway up my arms, and I didn't like being dependent on them. Regardless, life began to settle into a new routine, albeit much different than I had pictured in my childhood dreams.

My eighteenth birthday arrived, and I was finally walking upright without the sticks. I realized I needed a vocation, but my emotional development had been stifled and I was still floundering. Physical therapy had been important to me even though I had to leave the comfort of my home for three months to complete it. My physical limitations made the rigorousness of the work an unlikely chosen profession. I hid my anger from my family, but it was always lurking in the shadows.

One night while drinking in a bar with friends, I met the county commissioner for St. Louis County. At that time, I thought he was a political blowhard, but he was kind to me, and I never sensed anything nefarious about him. One evening, he asked, "I know a little about your dad and his business, and I don't understand why a nice and intelligent young woman like you is sitting in a bar wasting precious time?" Even through my hardened heart, his words struck a chord.

Using his vast connections, he made a call, and within a few short days, I was interviewing with the public health nursing department. I was hired on the spot as a nursing assistant. My boss, a compassionate woman by the name of Frances Clark, ran the program where I would work. I was taught how to do eye and ear examinations, and we were assigned to a school district where we would run tests on as many as twenty-five children a day. Our tests revealed that a high percentage of young children had unmet eye and hearing needs. We were committed to changing their world by ensuring they received the services they needed. I began to see how many people of all ethnicities were helped, which sparked an interest in me. I enjoyed being part of something much bigger than myself, and although my anger was gently pushed into the background while working with the children, it still dictated my decisions. Regardless, I was discovering the joy of serving people.

My boss became my friend. I called her Franny. After some time, we began to look for a change. It was decided that Franny, her youngest sister Katie, and I would apply at the State Department. It seemed exciting and filled with unique job opportunities as far away as Korea. We all applied. It didn't take too long to realize that I would not even be considered because of my polio. I was turned away, and feelings of anger rushed to the surface once again.

Katie, who could barely type thirty-two words a minute with forty-six mistakes, was hired with the understanding that she must first improve her typing skills. She asked me to help her, which I did, but inwardly I was seething. Here I was, an accomplished typist who could type at least a hundred words a minute with 100 percent accuracy, yet I wasn't even considered! Franny was hired immediately. She traveled to Washington, DC, to begin the thrilling process of working overseas as an embassy nurse. At this time though, the doctors discovered a nodule on her thyroid. Ultimately the nodule was discovered to be cancerous, and her dream of working in a faraway land was quashed.

Franny's cancer diagnosis was devastating to her. Faced with health issues, she had to rethink her next steps. Franny had inherited her parent's house, but she could not support it on her salary. She also felt responsible for caring for her older sister Mary Beth, who struggled with emotional issues. I wasn't interested in living in St. Louis any longer. I desired distance from the turmoil of my parent's divorce. We discussed many options but ultimately decided that all of us, Franny, Mary Beth, and I would share expenses and live together until such time as one of us met someone and married. This felt like a responsible economic decision. It was not an era where women comfortably lived alone or traveled without a companion. It helped that we all came from large families, which meant we were content with having many people around. Pooling resources, sharing expenses, and living together seemed like the perfect alternative for this time in our lives.

God, in His limitless wisdom, had other plans. I am reminded of Jeremiah 29:11 (NIV) when God says, "For I know the plans I have for you, declares the Lord, plans for welfare and not for evil, to give you a future and a hope." And wow did He have plans for me! I could not have imagined what God had in store. This was my first spiritual community and the beginning of my life's work. I just didn't know it yet. As part of my preparation, God began to work in my life. My eyes were being opened to the much bigger world around me. My focus was slowly shifting away from me and onto others.

We settled in Denver, and one Sunday morning while attending church at a large cathedral, I noticed a bum seated in the front row. I thought to myself, *What is that smelly bum doing sitting in the front row, and why is no one telling him to leave?* After church, I complained to Franny, "Why didn't the ushers remove him?" In Franny's gentle way, she responded with kindness, "It's cold outside, and many times, bums come into the church to be safe and warm." I responded, "But that's not right!" Again, Franny gently responded, "It's the one place that they know God will protect them." That hit me like a brickbat. "You really mean that?" I responded. It was the beginning of revelatory things for me to think about.

Life continued, and I was now working as a transcriptionist for crippled children's clinics all over the state. It felt like a course was set until I tripped and fell one day. I damaged my left ankle, which was already weakened by polio. The doctor said it might be time for me to consider warmer weather. Our little group had become my family, and we were all uprooted because of my polio! We chose Tucson, Arizona.

St. Mary's Hospital employed Franny and me. Franny was a nurse, and I was a medical transcriptionist. We were happy in this southern Arizona town. My mother was visiting because I was scheduled for minor surgery. I told my boss I was having surgery and needed three days off. Unlike in the past, I had begun thinking seriously about my life and desired to communicate honestly. My boss said no and further said that if I took time off, she would dock my pay. My adolescent reactions resurfaced, and I took time off anyway. To my absolute astonishment when I returned to work after three days, I was called into her office and told that my services were no longer needed. I didn't care. She had no right to treat me that way! I left in a huff!

At this time, there was also something significant happening in my life, which began to change everything for me and slowly altered how I viewed the world. I didn't fully understand my feelings, but I suspected God might be attempting to get my attention. While thinking about the change taking place within me, I remembered an encounter I had when I was very young.

At the age of twelve, I made what was called *a confession of faith* in an evangelical church. I stood at the front of the church, alongside all the other eager twelve-year-olds, ready to confess my faith in Jesus. I expected it to be a rather simple service, and we would all joyfully receive our certificates followed by a celebration with our families. Instead of blithely taking the certificate when it was presented and going on my way, I was instantly overcome with emotion. My heart felt like it was going to explode in my chest, my breathing was rapid and unpredictable, and my hands trembled. I was quite overwhelmed. The sensation was so intense that my family and friends began tilting their heads and curiously looking at me. Instead of celebrating at a nicely prepared luncheon, I was drowning in tears that continued for the next two days as I cried my heart out for reasons unknown. I came to the realization that this was my first encounter with the Holy Spirit. Little did I know that in two short years following this experience, everything I knew to be true and what I considered to be my greatest hopes and expectations would be shattered.

As I was maturing with a commitment to live in truth, the wounds of those early years and my hidden anger still lurked in the shadows. A major difference was that I had trusted prayer partners, and I began to open the wounded pieces of my heart and offer them to God for His healing. I faced my many unhappy years head-on by confronting everything that had created cavernous wounds in my heart.

During the years I struggled with polio, I only saw the disease as a major inconvenience. It was something to be loathed. As I shared my fears with God, I began understanding the lingering hurts I carried, and God started healing me. I realized that my anger resulted from my internalized fears: fear of sickness, fear of being alone, fear of abandonment, and fear for my future. These fears emerged as anger and sometimes rage. My sharp tongue was the most skillful weapon I possessed, and I used it forcefully in failed attempts to eradicate my fears. This was one of my unhealthy coping mechanisms.

During this time of healing, I learned that we could mark ourselves for life by the power of our words; if we allow it, others can also mark us, albeit sometimes unintentionally. Seeking God's forgiveness for ourselves and for those who have knowingly or unknowingly hurt us is the beginning of a transformed life. Seeking God's forgiveness was my beginning. I was no longer a *bull shooter*. I forgave my mother, Aunt Dorothy, and every family member who called me a name. My acknowledgment and forgiveness of everyone, including myself, removed the negative repercussions on my life. Just as Proverbs 18:21 NIV says, "The tongue has the power of life and death, and those who love it will eat its fruit."

My forgiveness provided me with a deeper discernment of the Word of God. God used all my experiences to teach me forgiveness, and forgiveness opened the door of grace for me to help others. I claimed God's word in James 5:11 (NIV), which states, "As you know, we count as blessed those who have persevered. You have heard of Job's perseverance and have seen what the Lord finally brought about. The Lord is full of compassion and mercy." With God's grace, I persevered. Through my perseverance, God readied me for my life's calling.

2

A SHOCKING
ENCOUNTER WITH
HOLINESS

IT WAS 1969. KATIE, Franny's younger sister, had an encounter with the charismatic movement. Although I was happy that I was becoming aware of God, I wanted nothing to do with anything that had a funny name attached to it or something that came with what I considered strange emotional behavior. Katie was relentless and kept encouraging us to look deeper. She insisted that we meet Mae Godfrey, a woman born and raised in Appalachia and living in Tucson. She asked us again and again to meet her. In an effort to get her to stop asking, we relented and agreed. I remember walking into her small, neat, and welcoming home. Mae greeted us at the door, her golden-red hair piled high on her head, and her Southern accent filled the room with warmth. After her gentle greeting, she said, "My friend told me you would like to hear about the Holy Spirit." It was one in the afternoon, and we sat down as she began to share.

Mae began sharing, "My story starts with my little boy. When my baby was four or five months old, my mother visited, and we placed the baby on a small blanket in the middle of the room. It was summer, and we were reflecting on how hot the days could get in Arizona. I noticed that my baby was perspiring, and his little curls were wet against his face. At that moment, I was so struck by the beauty that I said out loud to him, 'You are so beautiful that you must look exactly like the baby Jesus.' Well, that is what I thought I said anyway; however, the words came out completely unintelligible. I continued trying to speak, but absolutely everything I said sounded garbled. My mother stared at me with a confused look and a facial expression that indicated I sounded crazy. What was happening to me?

"By late afternoon, when these unintelligible sounds finally stopped, and I once again sounded like a normal human, I rushed to see my friend and pastor. 'What happened,' I asked. The pastor explained, in a calm tone, 'That was the Holy Spirit. Sometimes when people really love God, He gives them a new language to love and praise Him.'"

From that moment on, Mae explained that the Holy Spirit began working in her life, and she began to share stories with us that our hungry hearts were eager to hear. She explained that the more she prayed, the more people came to her asking for prayers. She would get calls in the middle of the night, fall on her knees, and begin praying until she felt the Holy Spirit say she could stop. She would dream of people and get up and pray, only to learn later from a friend that someone they loved had been in a serious accident and that they had been spared from injury or death. It was overwhelming and marvelous to listen to her.

During the Second World War, Mae continually dreamed about a man in an air force uniform. She knew he was American and could not understand why he was flying British planes. She would see planes dropping small black things, only later discovering that they were bombs. Some of those planes would be shot from the sky, and she would see black smoke rise from the ground. Her prayers increased, and so did her dreams.

She knew that when she dreamed about the American soldier, she was dreaming about a good man trying to end the war. There was one seriously damaged plane in her dream that was spewing smoke. It had been hit flying from France toward the English Channel. She continued to explain that she could see inside the cockpit and that there were two men inside. One man, who she assumed to be the pilot, said to the copilot that he should tell the other men to jump. The pilot was going to try to ride it out, but he wanted the men to be spared because he didn't know what would happen. She then saw five parachutes leave the plane with the pilot remaining inside. In the dream, she saw the young man as he frantically held onto the shaking controls, and she shouted out, "Save Kermit Bradford!" Mae continued to pray earnestly for the man.

Sometimes Mae's dreams would reveal locations. She saw a vision of Piccadilly Circus and Trafalgar Square in London, only to learn later that this area was where war intelligence information was picked up.

Many years after the war ended, she glanced out her window one summer day and saw her pastor's son running down the street waving a magazine in his hand. He was yelling, "Aunt Mae, Aunt Mae, my dad wants you to read this story." The magazine featured an article about a man saved from a plane crash during World War II. He said he never understood how the plane he was flying remained in the air after it had been catastrophically damaged and how he ultimately landed on his airfield. His name was Kermit Bradford. He was indeed an American. He had chosen to fight with England because America had not yet entered the war.

Mr. Bradford's long life had been richly blessed. He became a judge and later served on the Alabama Supreme Court. He was a solid Christian man who traveled the country teaching men about the love of God and the miracles of the Holy Spirit. We sat spellbound as Mae told story after story.

I now searched for God in a way I never knew was possible. Nothing mattered, not my parent's divorce, not my polio, no injustice, perceived or real, that had been done to me. I had been forgiven, and I had forgiven. The only thing that mattered was getting to know this God. This God of miracles.

We got the infilling of the mysterious Holy Spirit that day, and we wanted to learn more. Seeking God and learning His word was foremost for my journey. It wasn't always easy. I did not understand the path God had prepared for me then, and I am not sure I completely understood how ill-prepared I was. In my excitement, I wanted to rush out into the world to make a difference. Thankfully, God tempered my behavior and began leading me on a learning journey.

In some ways, I wanted to be like Paul. One could imagine that he wanted to rush into the world after his conversion, proclaiming God's love and healing power. After all, when you read his story as told in Acts 9:1–18 and retold by Paul in Acts 22:6–21 and Acts 26:12–18, it is easy to think that. After Saul sees a bright light flash around him, he falls to the ground, and hears a voice say, "Saul, Saul! Why do you persecute me?" He is blinded, and the Lord instructs him to go to Damascus where he would be told everything that God had determined for him to do. Saul followed God's instructions and found Ananias, who healed him of his blindness and baptized him, filling him with the Holy Spirit. After that, who wouldn't want to run into the streets proclaiming God's redemption?

If God could call Saul and rename him Paul from his ferocious persecutions of Christians and someone who was greatly feared, surely He can use me! The sun was setting after Mae's afternoon of sharing, and my learning journey was beginning.

3

THAT SHOCKING
FIRST MIRACLE

MY LIFE HAD TAKEN on a new direction. I hungered for God. It felt like a burning desire of unquenchable fire, yet life's negative realities remained unresolved. Starting my own transcription business, I had grown to love the doctors who always appreciated my work, but sitting in my little bedroom reminded me of being alone as a child. I referred to my room as the *jail cell*, and I was required to temper old feelings of restlessness. This time though, the feelings were superseded by something else. I wanted to know more about this God who consumed my thoughts.

I began to read my Bible. The more I read, the more I fell in love with the scriptures. I would often read until two or three o'clock in the morning. If I wasn't reading the Bible, I was reading recently published books about the Holy Spirit. I was enthralled, and my zeal was unending.

Franny and I joined a small gathering to share our faith. It was called a Catholic-Lutheran Living Room Dialogue. It wasn't designed to discuss the agreements or disagreements between our faiths but rather to spend time sharing our love of God. We met regularly and grew close as friends and as children of God.

Katie, who had accepted a position with the State Department, had returned from Tokyo. She felt and suggested to us that it was time we return to St. Louis and visit our families. The desert where we lived was dry and matched our meager salaries, so we could not afford to go together. We decided to take turns. Katie highly recommended that when we visit, we also attend a large prayer gathering. She said that we would learn even more about the Holy Spirit at this gathering. Katie and Franny's sister Barbara, who was a Catholic nun, were both involved in the group.

It was June, and we nominated Franny to attend first. When she returned, we anxiously asked, "What was it like?" Franny replied, "Wonderful." She explained how she had learned more about the Holy Spirit and God's love and that the priest had emphasized that God is still a healer. *Wow, really?* That was something for us to ponder.

While Franny was away, our friend Carol was due to deliver her third child. Franny had given Carol specific instructions not to have the baby in her absence. While Franny was flying home, Carol's husband began timing her contractions, and as soon as Franny's plane landed, I whisked her off to the hospital. We arrived to see a beautiful tiny baby boy tightly wrapped in a soft blue blanket, being held up to the window. The birth of this sweet baby was a blessing. We looked at each other, and inwardly we both realized it was time for us to get serious—very serious—about what we were doing.

Shortly after that, it was my turn to attend the prayer gathering. I arrived with nervous anticipation. The night of the meeting, Sr. Barbara carefully detailed how the evening would go. I felt a rush of apprehension when I heard the priest say, "This is a large group. Let's go around the room, and everyone can say their name and state why you came." I looked at Barbara and said unequivocally, "I am not doing that!" She smiled sweetly, gently patted my knee, and said, "That's OK. Don't worry."

The brief introductions were speedily taking place, and suddenly everyone turned and looked at me. To my astounding shock and dismay, with my heart pounding at approximately two hundred beats a minute, I shot up out of my seat and stated my name, "Marilyn!" Even more shocking, I announced that I had come to bring the Holy Spirit back to my friends! I quietly slid back down in my chair. I was in shock that I spoke out loud.

Following the meeting, individuals were invited to attend a Bible study or to meet in small groups for prayer. Barbara didn't give me much choice. I was going for a prayer. I silently asked God, "Please don't let me cry." For many of my childhood years, pride kept me from showing emotion during my sickness. I had become very averse to tears, and I certainly didn't want to begin trying them out now. A beautiful couple named Mr. and Mrs. McKee walked over to me and gently placed their hands on my shoulder. Immediately I began to feel the love of God. It was almost like a bomb had been placed in my chest and slowly exploded. This amazing sense of peace began spreading from my heart and through my entire body. I was completely immersed in love. One small tear dropped from each eye and rolled down my cheeks.

"Oh, Jesus," I silently said to Him, "I have known of You my whole life in one way or another, but I've never met Your Holy Spirit." I continued to sit quietly alone. The couple who prayed with me emphasized that I give God my tongue. I wasn't sure exactly what that meant, and it didn't feel normal or natural so I just let that thought pass. The sense of well-being was ever-present.

As I boarded the plane to fly home still filled with wonder about the experience of the weekend, I expected my usual fear of flying and the emotions that came with it to disturb my state of peace. However, when I boarded the plane on this day, everything was different. I looked out the window at the beautiful cumulus clouds forming in the sky, and as the plane soared over New Mexico, I realized I had been wondrously healed! I thanked God for what He did for me. By the time we landed, my whole world was new. Nothing was the same. I was a remade person, a new creation. I could hardly wait to share the immensity of my experiences with my friends.

It was the beginning of what was called the *charismatic movement*. Not everyone understood it. My brother-in-law teased me, expecting me to break out in song and dance at any given moment. In the past, I would have responded with anger at being teased. Now I didn't care that he chided me. My focus was on God and getting to know the Holy Spirit was the single most important endeavor of my life.

During this time, I was learning the distinction between the gifts of the Holy Spirit as identified in 1 Corinthians and the fruit of the Holy Spirit. The Bible speaks of both the gifts and the fruit of the Holy Spirit, and I had heard the words used interchangeably by Bible teachers. There is a difference though. I remembered an ancient, beautiful, and stately maple tree that grew in the yard of my childhood home. It helped me to reflect on the difference. The tree was noble and towering, and the branches were rife with foliage that provided much shade to everyone who sat under it. The large well-formed leaves that I admired represented the fruit resulting from a tenderly cared-for tree that had grown old with age yet remained strong and alive with a firmly rooted underground system of growth. With these deep roots, the tree bore much fruit. That is our role as Christians. We must allow a wellspring of Holy Spirit roots to firmly plant in the deepest part of our being to relish the fruits. The gifts are free, but to acquire the fruits, we must participate and mature in our faith.

As I was meeting people whose lives manifested one or more of the *gifts* of the spirit as identified in 1 Corinthians—knowledge, faith, healing, miracles, prophecy, distinguishing between spirits, speaking in tongues, and interpreting tongues, I grew in my faith and began to experience the fruit of the Holy Spirit. The book of Acts reveals seven fruits of the Holy Spirit: wisdom, understanding, counsel, fortitude, knowledge, piety, and fear of the Lord, and in Galatians 5:22–23 (GNT), we are told, "But the Spirit produces love, joy, peace, patience, kindness, goodness, faithfulness, humility, and self-control." That's a lot of fruit!

I will admit that initially when I heard miraculous stories of healing or other mind-blowing happenings, I was a little skeptical, and then as I witnessed more and more miracles, I grew quizzical. Why had I been the recipient of God's generous gift, and more importantly, what is my role going forward? On reflection, I could label this time in my life as *returning to school— Jesus style!* When I decided to follow Jesus, truly follow Him, I became a student and I am still a student. He is always teaching. God commands us to go into the world and use His gifts never leaving us empty-handed.

As I continued to voraciously read the scriptures, the Holy Spirit was beginning to reveal to me the delicious feeling of benefiting from the *fruit* of the Holy Spirit: the fruit that comes only from the Spirit of God. I could only attribute the joy and peace I felt even when my brother-in-law chided me as the result of the Holy Spirit dwelling within me.

Just like a beautifully tended garden that reaps a bountiful harvest, the Holy Spirit's fruits are available to us if we choose to do the work. A garden that yields a bountiful fruit harvest requires tending; the weeds must be pulled, plants need fertilization, and the vegetation must be watered. That is much like our walk with Jesus. When we invite Him into our lives and want healing, peace, or joy, we must commit to a daily strengthening of our spiritual walk through prayer, study, and community. We can all reap God's promise in Philippians 4:7 (NIV), "And the peace of God, which passeth all understanding, shall keep your hearts and minds through Christ Jesus."

Our small but ever-expanding group would meet weekly for prayer, and I was spiritually growing in the community. We were always amazed when unknown people of all faiths would show up at the door and say, "Is this the place for prayer?" They would enter and pray with us. Our numbers grew by the day and soon by the dozens. We were in awe and wondered at God and His marvelous ways.

One weekend, Franny and I attended a retreat at a center called Picture Rock. It was 1969, and while we were there, the local bishop's housekeeper asked if we would visit St. Mary's Hospital and pray with a friend of hers who was sick with cancer. We really didn't know any details, but we were moved by faith to say yes. We walked into the hospital room and realized that she was the only patient in the room. Her husband was sitting beside her with his head in his hands, distraught with grief. Her teenage son was standing at the side of the room, and it was easy to see that he was visibly upset and angry.

It felt like we were intruding. Franny was a nurse and had seen death many times. We looked at each other and wondered what we were doing there because clearly, this woman was at death's door. We began to step back to let the small family grieve quietly, but the patient slowly opened her eyes and beckoned us.

We told her that we were friends of friends and came to pray with her. In her weakness and extreme debilitation, she stretched out her hand and moved her head slightly up and down. Franny was on the left, and I stood on the right, each of us putting one hand in hers. I remember we held our other hands high, about shoulder length, in a praise position. As we began to pray, the near-death patient joined us.

I was amazed. I had never heard anyone pray like that before in my life. With her final breaths, she was praising God with a beautiful litany of love. Unexpectedly and without any warning, I felt what seemed like a bolt of lightning hit my arm and go through me, enter the patient through my hand, and leave the patient through her other hand before it entered Franny. She then released both of our hands. It was an astonishing and unnerving moment. At first, we had no idea what had happened!

Franny and I were new in this Holy Spirit prayer movement, and secretly, we thought we might have killed her. We exited the room as quickly as we could. We hardly said a word to one another all the way home. We thought we might need more lessons on how to pray with people.

The next day, we decided there was no need to go back because we were sure that this delicate woman had gone home to her Maker. The car had a mind of its own that day, and once again, we parked in the hospital parking lot and silently walked up to the dying woman's room. It was a beautiful day in early fall, and as we entered, we could see that the windows were slightly ajar. The curtains were gently blowing with the slight breeze that could be felt in the room.

We glanced inside and saw a woman with her feet dangling over the side of her bed eating her meal. We immediately exclaimed, "Oh, please excuse us. We have the wrong room." She excitedly looked at us and waved us back into her room.

After nine cancer surgeries and being imminently at death's door, she was now smiling. She was joyous, filled with strength, and thoroughly enjoying her hospital meal. She had been healed! This was the beginning of a blessed friendship gifted to us. Over the ensuing years, I would stop by her dress shop, where she would design clothes, and as she made beautiful creations on her commercial sewing machine, she taught me about the Holy Spirit.

I was learning a new lesson. God is never outdone in generosity.

As I continued to open my heart to God during this time, the scriptures became vibrantly alive within me. One evening during our prayer gathering, I was seated in a little chapel located in an out-of-the-way place called Sabino Canyon. I loved the intimacy of this chapel, and as I sat in the presence of the Lord, relishing in my love for Him and praising His name, I felt the Lord directing me to Isaiah 58:3–14. When I returned home later that day, I eagerly opened the passage and read God's word on true fasting. It was almost as though God lit up the chapter for me. I was powerfully impacted as I read,

> "Why have we fasted," they say, "and you have not seen it? Why have we humbled ourselves, and you have not noticed?"
>
> "Yet on the day of your fasting, you do as you please and exploit all your workers. Your fasting ends in quarreling and strife, and in striking each other with wicked fists. You cannot fast as you do today and expect your voice to be heard on high.
>
> Is this the kind of fast I have chosen, only a day for people to humble themselves?

Is it only for bowing one's head like a reed and for lying in sackcloth and ashes?

Is that what you call a fast, a day acceptable to the Lord?

Is not this the kind of fasting I have chosen: to loose the chains of injustice and untie the cords of the yoke, to set the oppressed free and break every yoke?

Is it not to share your food with the hungry and to provide the poor wanderer with shelter— when you see the naked, to clothe them, and not to turn away from your own flesh and blood?

Then your light will break forth like the dawn, and your healing will quickly appear; then your righteousness will go before you, and the glory of the Lord will be your rear guard.

Then you will call, and the Lord will answer; you will cry for help, and he will say: Here am I.

"If you do away with the yoke of oppression, with the pointing finger and malicious talk, and if you spend yourselves in behalf of the hungry and satisfy the needs of the oppressed, then your light will rise in the darkness, and your night will become like the noonday.

The Lord will guide you always; he will satisfy your needs in a sun-scorched land and will strengthen your frame. You will be like a well-watered garden, like a spring whose waters never fail.

Your people will rebuild the ancient ruins and will raise up the age-old foundations; you will be called Repairer of Broken Walls, Restorer of Streets with Dwellings.

"If you keep your feet from breaking the Sabbath and from doing as you please on my holy day, if you call the Sabbath a delight and the Lord's holy day honorable, and if you honor it by not going your own way and not doing as you please or speaking idle words, then you will find your joy in the Lord, and I will cause you to ride in triumph on the heights of the land and to feast on the inheritance of your father Jacob." For the mouth of the Lord has spoken. (Isaiah 58:3–14 NIV)

When I finished reading the miraculous words that were popping off the page, I experienced a profound interior moment. I knew God was using His scriptures to commission me and my dear sister in Christ Franny for our life's work.

Committed fully to what I felt was God's call on my life, I could hardly wait to share these important scripture passages with Franny. I responded with a resounding yes!

4

NOW THAT WE'VE MET, WHO WILL SHOW ME HOW TO FOLLOW YOU?

THE GATHERING OF THE Living Room Dialogue continued. We were also reaching out and beginning to share with other Christians the marvelous love of God and the power of His Holy Spirit. We received word one day that the husband of a young couple in the group, Richard, had a gallbladder attack and had been hospitalized. His recovery from surgery was not going well. In our enthusiasm, our group met regularly at the hospital to pray for his recovery although it looked bleak.

As we repeatedly sent our prayers heavenward without seeing much change, we didn't grow discouraged. We just prayed harder. One night, Carol said offhandedly to the group, "I believe God would do a miracle, but we need to know how to pray for it." That struck my heart because I wondered why she didn't think we knew how to pray for a miracle. I contemplated this for some time. The situation seemed so bizarre. It was a routine surgery, and despite our best efforts, the young husband did not recover. We all sat silently as we bade him farewell at his funeral the following week.

My friend's passing provided me with fresh spiritual insights. I was sad to lose a friend. I missed him, and I was disappointed because I understood that he would be unable to experience some of his life's heartfelt desires. While I felt saddened when I viewed his death through my natural eyes, I could also view his passing through my faith eyes. This was the gift that God gave me. I acknowledged that God had a different plan. I didn't know what it was then, but through unspoken faith, I discerned that God had heard every one of our prayers and had foreseen something better for my friend. I don't know what healing Richard received or what blessing God poured upon him at his death, but as it says in Hebrews 11:1 (NIV), "Now faith is confidence in what we hope for and assurance about what we do not see." I knew God had heard our prayers.

I trust in eternal life and know that we must first pass through this life to achieve it. I also recognize that we may not receive God's promises in this life. When Abraham journeyed to the mountain with his son, whom he was prepared to sacrifice at God's request, he remained faithful to God's promises. When Isaac said, "Where is the sacrifice, Father?" Abraham believed in the sovereignty of God and did not doubt God's promises, his faith did not leave him, and according to Romans 11, God fulfilled the promise He made to Abraham. He became the father of the nations, but through Abraham's natural eyes, it must have looked a little bleak to him at times.

We continued to forge ahead, and in alignment with God's perfect timing, which coincided with our need to gain even greater spiritual understanding, we learned that the sisters of

Canaan, a small group of Lutheran nuns, were coming to Tucson to speak. The sisters were joy filled. They lived the mission of repentance. The nuns were of German descent and had prayed diligently for the war to end. Now after the war, they felt it was their calling to pray for repentance, especially repentance for the sins of their country, for the Nazis, for the sins of all the people who participated in the genocide, and for the countless other atrocities of the war. They held a sincere belief that these humble prayers offered for their country would bring other people to receive knowledge of God and His goodness.

We eagerly attended their teaching, and shortly thereafter, we were blessed to attend a gathering the sisters held at their retreat sanctuary on the outskirts of Phoenix. The time we spent learning from them was filled with emotional moments and deep insights. They shared the gift of praying in tongues and helped us understand what a valuable gift it was for Christians to have this prayer weapon in their arsenal. The Holy Spirit was present in a mighty way. My adverse reaction to tears was beginning to change. Tears now revealed themselves to be tears of healing. I still didn't like them, but I was beginning to understand them. We were learning from these dear sisters how to strengthen our prayers and seek God's miracles in the world.

God gave us hearts of flesh, and we were filled with joy. We experienced the words in Ezekiel 11:19 (NIV), "I will give them an undivided heart and put a new spirit in them; I will remove from them their heart of stone and give them a heart of flesh."

Previously when I was told to pray in the Holy Spirit, my words sounded like gibberish, and I quickly disregarded it. Now I was beginning to understand that this is the gift Paul talked about in 1 Corinthians. I was learning that using this beautiful gift of the Holy Spirit strengthens our relationship with God and allows us to become more deeply connected to Him although frankly, I still wasn't sure if I knew how to do it. I had doubts about my ability.

One day while driving home from work, which meant I had to travel from the east side of Tucson to the west side, instead of my usual open dialogue with God and occasional singing, I felt like God was nudging me to speak to Him using His prayer language. The nudging was so persistent that I finally said to God, "I don't remember the words. Is that *really* you, God?" He reminded me of one of the words He had given me in an earlier encounter. The word was *ama*. I immediately had a flashback to my high school Latin class. That word means *He loves*. He gently reminded me, "Yes, that's right. I love you." His gentle spirit encouraged me to keep going. Suddenly more and more words formed on my tongue. I was excited! I didn't know what I was saying, but I knew that something inside me was enabling this gift's activation. I felt blissfully lifted and became happier and more joyous with each passing mile. What a ride home it was that day!

God confirmed in my heart that when we pray using the gift of tongues, the spirit within us is praying God's words. I loved my conversations with God, and now I absolutely love the Holy Spirit who uses His words to express His thoughts through me as an instrument.

I was searching the scriptures to understand more. Paul is explicit in 1 Corinthians that we can misuse our gifts as in all things good. The primary purpose is to have our own special prayer language to communicate between our Savior and us. It is the one time in our life when human foibles don't get in the way of communication. We are turning our most powerful tool, our personhood, and surrendering it completely to God for Him to use as He pleases.

My journey of learning continued to deepen in all areas of

my life. The nuns taught more profoundly about forgiveness, and their wisdom helped me as I committed to forgiveness at a deeper level. The instruction they provided showed me that what I thought I knew about mercy was only a drop in the bucket compared to what we receive from God. The nuns explained that while we may think that giving someone forgiveness was our gift to them, it was really a gift to ourselves. It was the basis for our own happiness and joy.

I considered these lessons. I realized how little I knew. If forgiveness is about our happiness, then why do we find it so difficult to embrace this gift of forgiving one another? Why in our misguided zealotry do we get so far offtrack and call our actions holy? I had a lot to learn. The sisters helped us realize that we could forgive as an act of will, yet if the unforgiveness remained in our hearts, and we continued to ruminate on injustice, we needed to take it to God again and sometimes again and again to receive a deeper level of healing.

We are instructed in 2 Corinthians to take every thought captive. When we choose to ignore this biblical directive and cogitate on perceived or what might even be a justified wrong, we become trapped by our emotions. Our unholy responses have the potential to become strongholds in our lives, and strongholds get in the way of spiritual growth. Feelings will *always* betray us, and when we dwell on them, we knowingly or unknowingly give the enemy access to us. We shouldn't ignore the circumstances that create an emotional response. Actions are real and impact us, but our responsibility is to consider the action, evaluate if we need to do anything, and move beyond it. Emotions like to take center stage, and with the enemy's help, they will even show off. I learned that we have a choice on how to handle unjust situations. We can respond to feelings of betrayal with anger, tears, gossip, and withdrawal, or we can surrender our emotions to God. When we surrender emotions, we open the pathway for God's healing.

If we want God's healing balm applied to our wounds, we must forgive. Jesus said to his disciples in Matthew 18:22 (NIV) when asked how many times they must forgive, "I do not say to you seven times, but seventy times seven." The nuns taught us that God did not want us to be afraid of how long it might take but rather come before Him expectantly over and over again as many times and for as long as it takes. This verse is important on another level. When Jesus says seven times seventy, the total is 490. In other words, according to Jewish tradition, it is never-ending. Forgiveness is a requirement to serve God. It is not an elective course at the local college. When we live in unforgiveness, we live an imperfect, incomplete life. When we forgive, we are given God's keys to expand our hearts and openly receive God's blessings. God is ready, willing, and wants to help us. We just need to ask. I was beginning to realize that God has more love than I could imagine through my limited lens.

As we began praying with many people, we were exposed to many hearts that had been utterly broken, often by other Christians. Even though they had struggled to forgive and said, "I forgive. I forgive. I forgive," the thoughts of these hurts or injustices would return, and feelings of pain would return. Many people over whom we prayed would often question if they had really forgiven since they still struggled with the old feelings of hurt and betrayal. God understands that the bruises of a lifetime do not go easily from our hearts. Our fallen nature wants to hold onto those bruises more than we need to and certainly more than we should. The relentless lover, our good Jesus, never gives up on us. We, too, should be relentless in bringing our hurts, sorrows, and all our bruises to Him even if it takes seven multiplied by seventy times.

God's astounding forgiveness is evident in the story of David, a man who genuinely loved God more than anything else in the world, but the scripture indicates that he had not surrendered all the areas of his life to God's authority. As a result, he committed a dreadful sin. The Bible tells us that he arranged the murder of his friend so he could marry his wife, whom David considered very beautiful. Even more tragically, he lusted after her, and she became pregnant with his child. He was with grief and cast himself on the *abundant mercy* of the Lord with his only hope of restoration from God (Psalm 51:1). The Bible says God forgave him. Ultimately David became one of the greatest kings of his time.

We came away from every encounter with a new understanding of what God really wants a Christian to be— seekers of forgiveness and generous forgivers.

Amid all our learning, we continued our nondenominational prayer meetings with other Christians. It was an exciting time because many people were returning to God, and groups were springing up throughout the country. People were contagious with their love for God. Unknown people would show up where we were gathered to pray, asking if they could join us. We welcomed everyone even though we often had no idea how they found us.

One evening we were at the home of a university professor and his wife, Walter and Dorothy Davis. Walt's dad had been a Presbyterian minister, and Dorothy's background was as a Quaker. Dorothy answered the door to a stocky, good-looking gentleman by the name of Elmer. Everyone took an instant liking to this new addition and greeted him warmly. Elmer came into our group with a seasoned prophetic voice. He had an aura of peace about him that was unmistakable. As the night ended, we joined hands and sang praises to God. Out of the corner of my eye, I saw Elmer break out of the circle and come up behind me. He leaned in close to my ear and whispered, "If you don't give the word that God has given you, I am going to have to do it."

What? My heart was racing at breakneck speed, and my knees suddenly went weak. Again ever so sweetly, he said encouraging words to me. After all these years, I don't remember the words I said, but I felt an immediate sense of relief when I began to speak. My heart settled, and I was filled with calm. That lasted for a few minutes, and then I had to sit down before I fell. I was overwhelmed with God's Holy Spirit.

That became the pattern. Elmer would float about the room using his mature prophetic gifts to teach the novices. God was using Elmer to encourage and teach us. Our prayer gatherings would end around ten o'clock, and we would sit and talk to Elmer often until one in the morning. He would share his vast knowledge of the scriptures and challenge us. He would say, "Don't take my word for it. Confirm it in the scriptures," and he would give us verse after verse. He never led us astray as he prepared us for our life's work.

Elmer helped us understand that one of the most misunderstood and often misused gifts of the Holy Spirit was speaking in tongues. Consider a new mother who tenderly cradles her infant and speaks in a language just known between the two. When we pray in the Holy Spirit, we are caught up in the love between the Father and Son, which releases God's power and healing. Romans 8:26 states, "In the same way, the Spirit helps us in our weakness. We do not know what we ought to pray for, but the Spirit himself intercedes for us through wordless groans." If you want this gift, simply ask God for it.

Elmer also shared with us that sometimes an individual may give the word, and it may not appear to turn out well. He taught us that after we give the word, it is not our responsibility to judge it. The person receiving the word can say, "I receive it," or they can reject it. Our responsibility was to listen to what the Holy Spirit was saying.

It was a beautiful time of learning, and I was always amazed at how God brought faith-filled people to us exactly when we needed it. Using people He brought into our lives, sometimes supernaturally, He provided three lessons during this time: the power of the gift of tongues, the power of forgiveness, and the power of the scriptures.

Many years later, our group was abandoned as a result of life changes; we were all living in different cities, and Franny and I had an occasion to meet with Elmer again. At this brief gathering, God, in His humorous way, gave Elmer and me the same word and asked me to nudge Elmer to give the word. God's wonderful sense of humor wasn't lost on me.

5

THE UNFOLDING JOURNEY

IT WAS AT THIS time we made a significant investment in our teaching materials. Notre Dame University had become one of the centers for the charismatic movement, and they had produced a series of lessons in the form of CDs about the Holy Spirit. We felt we needed to purchase these tapes for our learning and to benefit others.

The purchase of the entire series was slightly more than $200. At that time, Franny was making $310 a month, and I was making $210. It was a significant purchase for us, but we felt it was important. We were so committed that we decided to use the money toward this purchase when we each received our separate tax refunds. The tapes became an essential tool for our teachings.

During that time, we routinely visited the Benedictine Convent in Tucson, located just off Country Club Road. We enjoyed the beautiful grounds and loved spending time in adoration and prayer there. At that time, these beautiful edifices were available twenty-four hours a day, beckoning those who sought time with God in glorious and grace-filled surroundings.

One day a friend suggested that we share our teachings about the Holy Spirit with the nuns who resided on the grounds. We called and they were eager to learn more. We realized these nuns were beautiful in spirit and love when we met them. We began a warm and close friendship with them while sharing all we had learned about the Holy Spirit. Two of the nuns were blood sisters. They were small in stature, in fact quite diminutive but mighty in spirit. They embraced the teachings with eagerness, excitement, and enthusiasm. We began regularly holding Life in the Spirit seminars on the grounds.

One day Franny and I received a call from the two sister nuns. Almost breathlessly, they asked us to come over. We could not imagine what was weighing heavily on their minds, but immediately upon arriving, they began sharing. They had a brother who would soon be celebrating two important anniversaries—his fiftieth year as a priest and his twenty-fifth year as a bishop, now serving in New Guinea as an archbishop. They had been writing to him about everything they had been learning, and he wanted more information. He asked, "Is there anything in print?" This was the beginning of the Holy Spirit movement, and print material was sparse, but after one of our Life in the Spirit conferences, we packed everything extra and sent it on to him.

A few months later, the sisters called again. This time they said, "We need your prayers. Please come so we can share with you." By then the nuns were aware of the power of the Holy Spirit and were eager to enlist us in their prayer efforts. They explained that on their brother's upcoming dual anniversaries. He ardently desired to go to Rome and meet the Holy Father. Sadly he was a poor bishop without much money, and the prospects of making such a trip seemed particularly dim. The sisters, now fully schooled in the workings of the Holy Spirit, knew that anything could happen through prayer and with the Holy Spirit. Our community might have been a little more skeptical than the nuns although we didn't say anything to them. We agreed to join them in prayer. However, it did seem like a tall order.

At about that time, we had heard of a charismatic conference being held at Notre Dame University. Although Franny and I both wanted to attend, we had decided that once we started teaching together, if opportunities presented themselves, we would only take advantage of them if we could do it together so our learning would be aligned allowing us to grow together. We knew at that time that the cost of travel for both of us was out of the question, so we reluctantly dismissed the idea.

We continued working with our community—praying, teaching, and growing in the Holy Spirit. Franny had agreed to help one of our community members whose wife had surgery and contracted a staph infection while in the hospital. Her husband was very troubled about her extended stay in the hospital, so he asked Franny if she would be willing to take daily charge of all necessary protocols to keep the wound from getting infected if he was allowed to bring her home. Franny agreed and our friend reticently asked the doctor if he would approve the request. The doctor was unsure, but when he realized that Franny would be the nurse in charge, he agreed without a moment's hesitation. Her reputation was far-reaching. Of course, under Franny's care, the wound received daily blessings with holy oil along with prayer. It healed quickly.

A short while later, the husband learned, quite by happenstance, that the care Franny had given as a registered nurse qualified for payment. I answered the phone one day, and the husband asked to speak to Franny with the caveat that I should tell her that she had to say yes. Upon taking the phone, Franny learned that her care resulted in an unexpected payment of $600. In 1972, that was a windfall! We shouted for joy and whooped and hollered because we now knew that we could go to the conference, and we began making plans. Every detail along the way opened with abundant blessings.

While planning our departure, we received another breathlessly excited call from the sister nuns. "Please come! We have something to tell you," they exclaimed. Once again, we arrived curious as to what they had to say. We were astonished. The nuns explained that Quantus Airline, which had been a regional carrier, was expanding. The company's goal was to become a worldwide operation, and on their inaugural international flight, they wanted a few prominent people aboard the plane. The sisters happily shared that their brother was invited to fly first class (although they didn't know what that meant) to Rome, and from there, he could go anywhere he wanted. He chose Notre Dame University to attend the same conference we were attending!

Prior to the first evening of the conference, we had arranged to meet our Tucson contingent in a designated area of the stadium. Franny and I arrived early to watch for Abp. Alfred Noser, SVD, the brother for whom we had prayed. We sat down and asked God to help us find him in the crowd, and as God so often does, we looked up right before the conference began and there he was, standing right behind us. He greeted us with joy, and we were all able to share some personal time with him.

On the last day of the conference, he was the principal celebrant, present on the altar with approximately 150 other priests celebrating in the presence of the Holy Spirit. Shortly after the conference, we received a letter from the archbishop encouraging us to share this powerful information with the world. This is not a secret to be kept. This event taught us even more deeply the powerful gift of anticipatory faith, which the Old Testament so aptly explained.

By faith, we allowed the Holy Spirit to open our eyes to his purpose, giving us hope. The sisters lived with the expectation that God would answer their prayers, and their example impacted us. They fully embraced God's Word in John 1:12 (NIV), "Some, however, did receive him and believed in him, so he gave them the right to become God's children."

Their hope did something else. The seeds they planted about the Holy Spirit with their brother were given wings. The result was that the powerful training that we paid for with our pooled tax return money was sent across the world. We were able to see firsthand the importance of planting seeds that were allowed to germinate. What was an obedient response, which seemed a small gesture to us at the time, had a significant ripple effect on the kingdom.

The memory of our time at this conference, the lessons we learned, and walking up the steps to the sound of ten thousand people worshiping God in the mighty presence of the Holy Spirit will be forever seared on my heart with gratitude. Come, Holy Spirit. Fill the hearts of your people. As it says in Romans 8:1–7, it's a time to allow the Holy Spirit to spur you on to continue acting in faith.

6

THE DUMP

IN OUR CONTINUED PURSUIT of God, we attended many spiritual conferences. Katie, who had a beautiful gift of hospitality, would help bring speakers to the area, and we would receive firsthand knowledge as we would often share in the hosting of the speakers. At that time, we had been discerning a divine call in our spirits to form a new community. Part of our now rather large group, which included five married couples, felt called to begin a different work. They had purchased an old commercial tourist building to begin a ministry. Franny, Mary Beth, and another participant in our community, Carol, didn't feel called to that. We prayed for guidance. "Where did God want us to go?"

At about the same time, we attended a conference in California and heard a Catholic priest speak about the burning need for Christians to help care for the poor. His message spoke directly to our hearts. We prayed, we discerned, and we prayed even more. We considered moving to work with this priest in the El Paso area and at a place called The Dump, located just over the border. Ginny, Franny's sister and a Sister of Charity, had worked at The Dump for many years, which encouraged our decision to work there.

Before deciding to move to El Paso, we would sometimes visit. Every visit affirmed the need for the work. On one of our trips, I was asked to accompany some of the experienced prayer warriors in the area on their daily prayer rounds. Mrs. Tula, one of the group's leaders, explained to me that a woman with whom we would be praying that day was part of their regular visits. She further explained that this woman and her family had offended some of the people where they lived. The offense was so great that one day, an unknown person threw a cursed bag of powder into her apartment, striking her. She immediately fell to the floor and experienced what was later thought to be a stroke. At this point in our spiritual development, I was unaware of the bruja's (Spanish word for witch) spiritual power and influence, and that the *curanderos*, a Spanish or Latin American healer who uses folk remedies, would often extort money from locals in exchange for protection. I soon came to realize the malevolent power that was present.

When we arrived, Mrs. Tula tapped on the door, and we entered a very small and weathered apartment. My gaze was drawn to a small lady who was strapped to a fragile kitchen chair with a piece of material to keep her from falling. She immediately recognized my companions and smiled sweetly. We all knelt around her and began to pray. Mrs. Tula said to me quietly, "Marilyn, if the Lord gives you a scripture, please read it." I opened my Bible, and my eyes fell on Psalm 9. I was quite sure this delicate and obviously quite ill woman did not understand English, and I did not know how to read the words in Spanish. I read them, nonetheless, "The Lord is a refuge for the oppressed, a stronghold in times of trouble. Those who know your name will trust in you, for you, Lord, have never forsaken those who seek you. Sing praises to the Lord enthroned in Zion; proclaim among the nations what he has done."

I finished reading the words, and Mrs. Tula encouraged me to read the scripture again. This time she said, "Please do not stop reading until the Lord tells you to." It's difficult to suppress our natural feelings at moments like this, but I trusted Mrs. Tula and her experience. I did as she said. Over and over for at least fifteen minutes, I read this powerful passage from Psalms. I am not sure if I can tell you how I knew it was time to stop reading, but when I did, I fell silent. I looked up to see this frail woman, tied to the chair, began to weep profusely. She then lifted her once paralyzed arm and placed it around my neck, saying repeatedly, "Gracias, a Dios. Gracias, a Dios. Gracias, a Dios." Thank God. Thank God. Thank God.

I was overwhelmed by what I had just witnessed. The woman had been healed. Like the tiny lady in the chair, I responded repeatedly, "Thank you, Jesus. Thank you, Jesus. Thank you, Jesus." That small kitchen was filled with the love and light of Jesus Christ.

This was my first experience witnessing the healing power of the Word of God. In the many years since, I have seen the power of God's Word healing physical and emotional issues that held people captive for years. Claiming the Word of God releases God's power.

By then we knew that we desired to move to El Paso, but we were not sure it was feasible. At that time, the housing market in Tucson was in disarray, and the economy was sluggish. In the area where we lived, there were at least 200 tract homes with For Sale signs on them for months. Hughes Aircraft, one of the largest employers in the area, had laid off many of its employees.

It did not look promising that we could sell our house. Franny finally said, "Well, that's our test." If we sell the house, then we know we should move.

I shouldn't be surprised when God answers a challenge; nonetheless, we were surprised. The home that Franny, Mary Beth, and I shared, which we purchased for $11,000, was sold within twenty-four hours for $26,000. Carol's home sold within twelve hours for $30,000. It all happened so fast that we had to initially leave Franny behind to complete the paperwork. Carol drove her car with her four sons inside, and off we went. We only took the living room couches and chairs because we knew we would need them.

Our life of worship through hands-on service began.

Ginny found a beautiful large home on the street called Rio Grande for all of us to share. It had a large living room at least thirty-five feet long with the most beautiful carved doors in the hallway. The upstairs was beautifully finished with a fireplace on each side. There was a lot of space for everyone to serve God in this new environment with spacious rooms to welcome people in desperate need of God's love.

The priest we heard speak had been doing formidable work at The Dump. He told us that when he was originally deployed to work there many years ago, he was walking through the area and witnessing firsthand the abject poverty, the numerous bars, the extreme filth in which people lived, and the utter sense of hopelessness. While on this private personal assessment tour, he noticed a woman in a dark and menacing alley. She had just delivered her baby. When this young woman saw his white collar, she immediately knew that he was a priest, and she hysterically cried out to him while holding her infant. Her baby had just died. It was a moment of reckoning for him. He was grief-stricken. Later he would share with us that this shocking instant forever changed his life because he felt overwhelmed with a feeling of hopelessness. Therein began his life of service to these humble and neglected people.

When we arrived, everyone was delighted to have new recruits. There was a lot of work to do at The Dump and in El Paso, and we were eager to serve.

Prior to our arrival, God strongly impressed upon me that I should set up parameters for regular discussions with the church leader about our work. This troubled me. I was grateful that we would be working under a priest's direction. For once, I was not in charge. Personally, I did not want to take up the leadership mantle again. I had heard God clearly and knew what He was asking me to do, but I resisted. In total disobedience, I ignored God's request, a decision that I would later deeply regret.

Among my tasks was the responsibility of Bible studies for the people. My love of the scriptures and my continued studies, still reading the Bible until two or three o'clock in the morning, was a role that I was excited about. The people in the area were hungry for the Word of God, and I loved teaching and sharing it. Franny was asked to work directly with the people living in The Dump, putting her notable nursing skills and genuine love of God to work.

We also had full-time jobs. I worked as a medical transcriptionist, and Franny was a nurse at the local hospital. Life was full and fulfilling. I treasured the opportunities I had to teach the Bible, and I was amazed that even when an interpreter wasn't present, the Bible would cross the language barrier as the Word of God became alive.

Franny would come home and share amazing stories of healing and hope that occurred at The Dump. These stories encouraged me and those attending the Bible studies. We were blessed to witness in real time the living truth of God's promises as found in the scriptures.

Her stories were stunning. She shared with us about a tender and somewhat anxious Hispanic priest named Fr. Madrid. Franny was asked to be his escort when he visited The Dump. Fr. Madrid was uncertain about how to interact in such bleak conditions. The needs of the people were so extreme. He questioned Franny, "What should I do?" Franny, who was always gentle, replied, "Just love the people."

It didn't take long for Fr. Madrid to get his working introduction. As he emerged from the parked car, exiting on a pile of rubbish, a lady ran up to him holding her young child, "Padre, por favor, por favor. Padre, por favor." Franny immediately noticed that the young child had a club foot. The infant's foot was turned inward so severely that the bottom of the foot faced upward. Franny, who by now was quite experienced praying with people in need at The Dump, said to the priest, "Oh, Father, the madre wants you to pray for her baby." He awkwardly took the child in his arms and following Franny's instructions began praying for healing while gently placing his hand on the baby's ankle. Instantly, the baby's foot was healed. Instantly! The priest was so shocked that he almost dropped the baby. He was overwhelmed by God's healing, and from that day forward, he worked faithfully with the people and loved working as a team with Franny.

As Franny was leaving our community house for The Dump one day, she announced that she would take Carol's four boys along with her. She felt they should be exposed to people in need and offer assistance to the poor. I was very apprehensive about her decision. I suggested that it might be hard for her to track not one but four boys at the same time. Franny was confident that it was the right decision.

As Franny and her group of ducklings walked up to the people, they discovered a small house made of trash and cardboard against the hill with a Mexican woman inside. Franny could tell she was having a seizure. She immediately gathered the boys and said, "Come on, let's pray. Put your hands on her as we pray." The boys were having trouble adapting to these strange circumstances as the woman's body and face were covered with flies, but Franny insisted and said to the boys that they should just thank Jesus. They complied. Once again our great God came through.

Instantaneously the flies flew away, and the woman sat upright. The young boys got to see God's miraculous answer to prayer up close and personal that day! Franny never doubted.

Our work together deepened my friendship with Franny. Everything that I was—sometimes impatient and struggling with discontent in the early years—Franny helped balance with her gentle spirit and compassionate heart. Franny served an audience of one, and that one was God.

Franny loved the people at the border. She applied all her compassionate nursing skills toward them. Eventually word spread of how the people who lived in these squalid conditions were receiving help. The word was spreading so rapidly that the information reached the ears of the president of Mexico. He wanted to see for himself and scheduled a visit. He showed up on the appointed day with his security detail in tow, looking quite magnificent. My schedule prevented me from meeting the visiting dignitary and his entourage, but Franny and another good friend of ours, Jeannie, were present to explain the assistance being provided to the people.

Franny and Jeannie returned home later that day to tell me about the experience. When Franny was out of the room, Jeannie said she was amazed by how Franny handled herself. Jeannie said that it was clear that Franny was at The Dump to serve the people and paid no attention to the visiting dignitary other than to warmly shake his hand and thank him for visiting. I smiled because I knew in my heart how true that statement was. Moreover, I thought Franny probably didn't even pay attention to who was visiting. She was there to serve. When Franny returned to the room, I asked her, "Franny, are you aware of who visited The Dump today?" She said, "Oh yes, those wonderful people formed a group and appointed a president to represent them." That was Franny.

As time went on, we began to see changes in the environment that made our small group grow troubled. I wrote earlier that I ignored God's request to ensure that our group had scheduled times to regularly dialogue in a meaningful way about how things were going. Had I followed God's instruction, we would have communicated frequently about everyone's needs and understood points of view about the ongoing activities of the work. As the ministry evolved and challenges occurred, there was no trusted place to discuss misunderstandings.

I learned that even in God-seeking communities, discord can occur. Even though Paul had a watershed, earth-shaking moment when the Lord spoke to him on the road to Damascus, he still had disagreements with the other apostles. These disagreements did not derail Paul's ministry even though Paul states in Galatians 2:11 (NIV), "But when Peter came to Antioch, I opposed him in public because he was clearly wrong." The early Christians did not allow grudges to fester. Instead, they created an environment where they could discuss and when necessary, forgive in love. Sadly in many Christian communities, disagreements lead to a separation among believers and hinder everyone's spiritual development. This is what happened in our situation, and we knew it was time for us to leave. It caused Franny and me crushing personal grief.

I blamed my disobedience for our departure from El Paso. God had given me the gift of leadership, and with this gift came responsibility regardless of who is involved in the community, including other spiritual leaders. I abdicated my responsibility to stand in truth as stated in Ephesians 6:14 (NIV), "Stand firm then, with the belt of truth buckled around your waist, with the breastplate of righteousness in place." God showed me through this experience the importance of obedience and how disobedience potentially interferes with God's plan. Whenever God asks us to do something, it is always for our benefit. We departed El Paso. I trusted that God generously gave me the forgiveness I asked for, but we were brokenhearted when we left.

This was a significant lesson for me. There are many biblical stories about the cost of disobedience, beginning with Adam and Eve, Cain and Able, Lot's wife, and the destruction of Sodom and Gomorrah, just to name a few. These challenging stories are found in just the first two books of the Bible.

We can read those stories and think to ourselves, "Oh, I wouldn't do that." I certainly thought that way. Yet every day, we are faced with the decision to choose God and His will or choose our desires. Our responses might show up as partial obedience, questioning, or responding with frustration or annoyance. Sometimes we may even bargain with God. All God asked of me was a simple yes. I put my faint-hearted needs first, based on what I wanted, and my decision to ignore a basic instruction resulted in an outcome that affected me and others.

Upon our leaving, the enormous delight of the work was momentarily eclipsed, but it did not take away from the powerful work that was accomplished before or after our departure. God, in His infinite generosity, healed our hearts completely although it did take time and created unnecessary angst. God really does know best.

7

WHERE DO WE GO
NOW, LORD?

UPON LEAVING, FRANNY AND I knew that it would be important to take time to reflect on our experiences in El Paso and discern what God was calling us to do next. We had heard about a two-week conference in San Antonio, which Fr. George Montague was leading. He was a nationally known scripture scholar. We quickly signed up. We wanted to be students among praying people seeking God's will. The charismatic movement was growing strong throughout the country, and these conferences attracted many people in search of God's glory.

We arrived at St. Mary's University campus ready to soak up the Body of Christ in this wonderful milieu of people. We arrived early, and rather than tour the campus, we sat in the chapel, preparing our hearts. As I settled in, I noticed a beautiful wool tapestry of the Last Supper hanging on one of the side walls. This tapestry didn't just catch my eye. I was drawn to it as though there was nothing else in the room. I studied the faces of the apostles, all looking lovingly at Jesus, and then I noticed Judas. He too was seated at the table, but he was separated from Jesus by the space of a person, and he was the only apostle not looking longingly at Jesus. Instead, his face was turned away. My heart was burdened, and I wondered, *Did we just separate ourselves from the body of Christ?* I looked at Franny sitting in a different part of the room, and she too was weeping. It felt like time stood still.

As painful as this experience was for me, I knew that God was with me in my suffering. God understands suffering. He emptied His heart of the very last drops of blood and water for us. He gave it all. On the way to the cross, He held nothing back. God understands betrayal, disappointment, hurt, grief, and rejection because He also experienced it. He understood as I cried out Psalm 86:5–7 (NIV), "You, Lord, are forgiving and good, abounding in love to all who call to you. Hear my prayer, Lord; listen to my cry for mercy. When I am in distress, I call to you, because you answer me."

After a long while, the choir entered the room to practice for the beginning of the conference. They began singing a new Hosea song titled "Come Back to Me with All Your Heart." We continued to sit in silence with our tears for at least another hour as the tranquility of the chapel and the uplifting voices of the choir ministered to our hearts.

When we met later for dinner, our spirits had been lifted, and we were anticipating the conference. When Fr. George came in and began to share the word of God, our hearts burst open, and the healing process began through God's powerful words. The next two weeks were filled with blessed fellowship and instruction from the scriptures. Unlike many of the miracles we had seen, my emotional healing was not instantaneous. The process was sometimes slow and occasionally painful, but it was steady. Once again, we were asking, "Where now, God?"

Our friends, the Galindos, had been asking us to come to Phoenix, so we decided to visit. After we arrived, they invited us to meet some of the people in the Hispanic community where they had been working. Feeling as though this was where God was calling us, we secured an apartment in the same area as our friends. We began conducting weekly classes in South Phoenix. We were counting on the Lord's help, especially with anyone who needed translation from English to Spanish because we were not bilingual. We trusted God.

Our group started small, maybe twelve people. We shared some of our journeys and asked them to share their experiences. We quickly realized that many of the people participating had experienced significant trauma in their lives. Sadly many of these dear people had reached out for help, often to people using Jesus's name but not His scriptures. Additionally, they added their manmade teachings, which left many confused and sometimes with negative feelings toward God. Many had been frightened by the misguided teachings of the Word they received.

During this time, we began to understand why we were there. As people came to us, often privately for prayer, we would learn their stories. There was a pattern of abuse, neglect, abandonment, and addiction. The list was long. They were willing to do the work to get healed; they just didn't know how to do it.

It was our responsibility to share the truth of the Word of God and how healing is possible through Jesus's mercy. The number of people who came to pray grew and then grew some more. People came for healing and in search of answers for their life. How could *they* hear from God? How could they or a family member be healed from the effects of alcohol, drugs, addictions, and immoral relationships? People came from all over—many from out of state. People were searching for the truth.

Our teachings were now very systematized. The tapes we had purchased from Notre Dame while living in Tucson were central to our teachings. Our classes began with a formalized introduction of a godly concept using one of the tapes, followed by a discussion based on the scripture. They ended with personalized prayer over everyone present. We continued to outgrow our space as we moved from one house to a bigger house. Miracles abounded.

As people opened their hearts and began their healing journey, it influenced their families, frequently causing disruptions in their households. More members of the same family would eventually come until a complete household had placed their trust and faith in God.

At this time, there were several committed supporters of the ministry who believed it would be prudent to establish a nonprofit to facilitate outreach activities. We formed a small board of directors and applied for a 501(c)3. Everyone told us we would have to wait for months for anything to be approved. Much to everyone's delight, the paperwork was received, and our newly formed nonprofit was official within three weeks.

We had named it the Institute for Human Development and the work began. The name was mighty, but the work was simple. We trusted God to intervene in the lives of everyone who came through our door. Franny and I were always present to lead in prayer, and many others would join us as their schedule permitted.

God did many amazing miracles during those years. We would witness enormous mind-blowing miracles, and we would also see God's tender healing mercies. He granted exactly what someone needed when they needed it. Maybe it was the gift of forgiveness, strengthening one's faith, or a renewed outlook on a painful situation. It was marvelous to be used by God in this powerful way, always knowing that we were just the instruments. Our resounding *yes* to God allowed Him to touch many, and just like the grace that fell on Simon when he carried the cross for Jesus, we were continually blessed by that same grace.

Sometimes people would come, and the situation seemed so bleak that my humanity would creep into my thoughts. I would wonder how God could ever fix certain difficult situations. He never failed.

One such experience was a young couple who came to us due to complications with their yet-to-be-born baby. The mother had miscarried their first child, and the sorrow and overwhelming desire for a baby were heavy on their minds. She had gotten pregnant again, and they had just breathed a sigh of relief when the first trimester safely passed, but they soon learned that they were not out of the woods yet—far from it! Through a routine exam, the doctor explained that their precious baby's brain was not developing normally. Further specialists were needed.

With fear and great anxiety, they made an appointment to meet with a pediatric neurosurgeon and other advanced practitioners. It was then they learned their infant's brain was abnormal. The fourth ventricle did not close; fluid was accumulating in the head. This fluid prevents the cerebellum from developing and enlarging the size of the baby's head. The stricken parents were told that their infant would have severe brain damage, and the chance of survival was in question. The statistics were grim. Fifty percent of babies diagnosed with this condition pass away within a short time after birth, 25 percent are severely handicapped, and the remaining babies experience a range of disabilities.

They were filled with grief and questions and overwhelmed about what lay ahead of them, so they went into prayer.

There were so many prayers. Prayers for healing, prayers for not delivering too soon, prayers for the baby's eyesight, and prayers for the infant to be able to eat. The list was long. It was a bewildering time. Prayers and novenas were sent up to heaven on a regular basis by caring family members.

In this young mother's quest for help, she was told about our prayer gathering. She called and asked, "May I come?" We scheduled a time, and she later shared that upon her arrival, she immediately felt the warmth and comfort of the loving and prayerful people. She told her story to the group, who began praying intensely.

At that moment, the young mother later explained she felt very close to God as He revealed His presence to her, and she began to understand how much He truly loved us and how He walked with us even through heartbreaking circumstances. It is easy to blame someone, especially God when something tragic happens. She said, "I completely understood God was with me in this circumstance." The young mother went on to explain that the prayer became so intense that at one moment she felt like she was going to faint, yet simultaneously, she was at peace. Someone in the group explained that this was the Holy Spirit. It was an amazing experience for her, and she was filled with gratitude. She began attending this prayer group weekly and felt stronger and more at peace each week.

During the thirty-seventh week, a beautiful perfectly formed baby boy George entered the world. Four hours after he was born, the doctors ordered an MRI. As they predicted, the cerebellum had not developed. George was in the neonatal ICU for twelve days, during which he had two surgeries. Before his discharge, the doctors ordered another MRI to make sure the shunt that had been placed inside his head during one of the surgeries was still in the proper location. To the doctors' amazement, there were signs that George's cerebellum was growing!

The parents assumed that because everything was going so well, the diagnosis must be very mild, but when they asked the doctor, he reassured them that George had a very severe diagnosis. They began what they thought would be a long, arduous process with outcomes unknown. The shunt was revised three times during a short three-month period. Each time an MRI was taken, there were more signs that George's cerebellum was forming. Much to everyone's shock, a membrane was developing.

This news made everyone—parents, family, friends, and prayer warriors—rejoice in God's blessing!

That fall, the doctor ordered another MRI to determine the shunt's position. If the shunt had shifted and required adjusting, it would mean another dreaded surgery. Everyone waited. The doctors finally returned to give a report. They said they were stunned and in joyful harmony, "George has a normal healthy brain, and his cerebellum is completely developed." The shunt was removed. Repeatedly and still in joyful harmony, they said, "This is amazing! We have never seen this before." Everyone knew God had performed a miracle, which strengthened everyone's faith.

8

GOD TAKES US
EVERYWHERE

OUR LITTLE GROUP WAS now deeply focused on teaching about the healing spirit of God as the scriptures detail in 1 Corinthians 12. People were hungry to learn about God and excited to discover that He is as present today as He was in the Old Testament. People came from all over the Valley. Two or three times a week, guests would show up at our door representing many different Christian denominations: Catholic, Baptist, Methodist, Presbyterian, and Lutheran. Being a member of a denomination did not safeguard against hurt, disappointment, or disease.

The days and nights were eventful with a robust telephone ministry and personal one-on-one ministry in homes. We often had to change locations to accommodate the many searchers of truth. A pattern emerged. Everyone who came to pray wanted to know more about this wonderful God we talked about, and when people showed up with their lifetime of hurts and disappointments, they also brought a desire for healing. Most importantly, they brought hope. They came with something else that was equally important. They had the willingness to do whatever was necessary. This is what I would fondly call *the work*. The work included everyone looking deeply into their hearts to find forgiveness for everything they had experienced and the willingness to change their behaviors if that was required.

Franny and I worked full time, so there wasn't much time left in our hectic-filled days, but we considered ourselves blessed. Although we had set up a small nonprofit, we never charged anyone, and God always provided.

One night we received a call from one of our dear friend Egeu Baretto. He was a well-respected, deeply loved cardiologist who had helped us get established in our work. He was the embodiment of a Christian leader. He was filled with wisdom, gentle with everyone he encountered, and faithfully embraced discipleship. He asked us to meet him at the Hyatt Regency downtown for dinner. Of course, we were delighted.

Egeu met us in the lobby and introduced us to a friend of his who had just arrived from Brazil. Her name was Anita. She needed surgery on her knee and could not find the necessary therapeutics in her country. Our friend encouraged her to come to the United States and receive the treatment she needed under his watchful eye. We had a lovely dinner in the distinctive revolving rooftop restaurant while watching the lights of the city. Our guest was fluent enough in English that we could communicate without a need for translation. Franny and I noticed that Egeu's guest ate very little, but we also knew that she had flown on multiple connecting flights culminating in eighteen hours of travel. We assumed she was tired.

Before we departed for the evening, we confirmed the arrangement to pick her up at the small out-of-the-way hotel where she would be residing during her treatment. The following morning, I had to be at work by six o'clock, which meant that Franny would pick up Anita to take her to her first appointment. We discussed Franny stopping by a lovely twenty-four-hour French café that we both liked so she could bring Anita some coffee and a light breakfast. We knew that by now, she would probably be ravenous. When Franny arrived at Anita's door with the breakfast goodies, Anita took what was offered, and her eyes filled with tears. She later explained to us that this was the first time in her life that a genuine gesture of love was offered to her without expecting anything in return. Christian love moved her deeply and started the process of healing.

We began to learn more about Anita and her life in Brazil. Anita's mother was born in Germany, and shortly after her birth, she was adopted and raised by a prominent German family. The family saw the potential in the beautiful country of Brazil, and as early as 1900, they began developing seaports there and moved to that country. After Anita was born, her mother would travel back to her country of origin each year with her and her sister along with the family's maid to visit the remaining relatives. A short while before the terror of Hitler began and the war commenced, one of Anita's visits instilled a long-lasting fear into her mind. The family had been quietly enjoying their time away when much to their surprise, an uncle, a general in the German army and part of the plot to assassinate Hitler, crept quietly into their guest quarters. He firmly instructed his visiting family, "Leave immediately. Do not take anything. One more ship is leaving tonight, and you must be on it. Do not come back!" They did as they were told and left for the port immediately, anxious and fearful. When they arrived, they found the port packed with people screaming. It was the night of Kristallnacht, or what was often called the Night of the Broken Glass.

That night, a pogrom against Jews was being carried out by the Nazi party's paramilitary forces. The name Kristallnacht comes from the shards of broken glass that literally covered the streets after the windows of Jewish-owned stores, buildings, and synagogues were smashed. Everything was attacked, and over 7,000 many Jewish businesses were ultimately damaged or destroyed. It was a terrifying night and even more terrifying through the eyes of a child.

They left by boat, and by the first day at sea, they had reached deep water, and the family was still reeling from what they had witnessed. The small group emerged from their room, and an unidentified seaman aboard the ship frenziedly rushed up and grabbed Anita, gripping her and hanging her over the rail, screaming at the top of his voice, and threatening to throw her overboard. Anita became frightened and had a panic beyond anything she had ever experienced. Before the seaman could drop her into the icy cold water, another man appeared seemingly from nowhere and rescued her. Even as Anita matured into a lovely and talented woman, this experience left her feeling wounded and fearful.

The routine gesture of offering a hot coffee and light breakfast symbolized something much more significant. It was a gesture of love. Anita began to open her heart during her stay with us, and we were touched by her vulnerability. We invited her into our home for the remainder of her visit, and everyone in our group helped to provide transportation, prayer, and random acts of kindness. During her visit, we celebrated her birthday in true commemorative style.

Anita would weep at the generosity of Christians who expected nothing in return. We prayed with her, discussed many of her sad experiences, and read the scriptures, and God did His sweet work of loving her back to wholeness through His people. We were honored to be used by God.

The day arrived for her departure, and we knew saying goodbye would be difficult. She made us promise that we would someday visit her. We weren't sure how that could happen on our limited budget, but we knew that if God wanted us to work in Brazil, He could make that happen. We continued a sweet relationship through cards and letters.

It was probably three years later that Egeu called one night and said that he and Phyllis, his wife, wanted to come and visit us. Of course, we invited them. He prefaced his visit with the statement, "You can't say no." We were uncertain as to what that meant. He arrived and immediately arranged the chairs around the fireplace, which created a cozy circle for all of us to enjoy. He then presented us with a check from Anita and her family. The money would make a visit to Brazil possible for Franny and me. When I saw the amount, I said it was too much money, but our good friend assured us that Anita wanted us to have every penny with permission to use whatever we needed to prepare for our first international trip.

Franny and I decided we didn't want to show up as uneducated Americans, so we signed up for a three-month course to learn how to speak the language. I can't say that we were flamboyantly capable, but ultimately, we could negotiate our way through simple things. Franny could speak it better than me, and I could understand it better than she, so we managed quite successfully between the two of us.

The trip was filled with God's blessings. We were able to pray with kindhearted Brazilians and celebrate many occasions with Anita's beautiful family. During our one-month stay, we flew all over the country, sharing God's love in the countryside where the poorest of the poor lived.

This was our first international trip. God showed us that He was not limited by our thinking. All that was required was our *yes* to serve. This was our first, but not our last, trip abroad. God had more overseas travels planned for us. Although we never knew God's ultimate strategy at the time, we always looked back and saw the spiritual growth that resulted from the experiences that were provided to us.

Our community had come together in remarkable ways, and the closeness of the group was something relatively new in my life. Individually and collectively, we were searching to know God in deeper and more intimate ways, and we found that through sharing our lives with each other, our relationship with God deepened in miraculous ways.

We were presented with the opportunity to visit the birthplace of our Lord, Jerusalem. There were six of us that decided to make the journey. The group included Egeu, Phyllis, and another couple with whom we had grown quite close, along with Franny and me. We were blessed to have a seasoned tour guide who had led many groups previously and shared a spiritual friendship with Egeu and Phyllis.

Upon arrival in this foreign yet oddly familiar land, we exited the airport and looked up at the towering palm trees with real live camels waiting below them. We were reminded that this scene decorated many Christmas cards we had received or sent through the years. Scenes like this were constant reminders of our affection for this strange land.

There was something else that happened, and it was something that everyone in our little group experienced. I got an overpowering sense of "coming home" when I set foot on the sacred ground of the land where our Lord resided. I was filled with a sense of harmony unlike I had ever known. With this incredible sense of *belonging*, we boarded a fully packed bus with eager American tourists. In addition to the traveling tourists, there was a tour guide from another company returning to

Bethlehem. His name was Joseph, and the irony of this handsome young man's name returning to his birthplace of Bethlehem was not lost on me. It was nightfall as we drove through the city to the hotel, which meant our sightseeing was somewhat limited, but regardless, Joseph began sharing details of the area and we were enthralled. We passed through a large community in Israel that began in the early 1900s called Kibbutz. These were created to help restore the land. We could hardly contain our anticipation for the days ahead!

We rested that evening with the sounds of air raids and the noise of occasional bombs, but we were assured that we were traveling under the protection of the Israeli government and we had faith in them. Nothing could deter us from the enthusiasm of being in the land where Jesus was born.

Our pilgrimage began officially the next morning. Our first stop was to visit the place where Jesus suffered his crucifixion. The bus parked at the edge of the area, and our group within the larger group exited the bus together. We were walking on the cobblestone streets of Old Jerusalem, and as I came closer and closer to the church, which was our first stop, I was overcome with emotion in a way that I still can't express today. Every cell in my body was heavy with the weight of the cross, and I dissolved into tears. I was stopped dead in my tracks. My friends would come back and encourage me, but I stood still. My dear friend Egeu eventually guided me up the stairs although as I recall, he had to practically carry me. I continued to cry. The entire experience of being in this ancient land filled me with emotion and created a literal waterfall of tears. My group of close confidants was kind and loving, helping me along in a very tender and sweet way. I finally said to God, "I am not sure I can do this trip for two weeks. This is exhausting."

Later that same day, we were going to walk the Via Dolorosa, often translated as the Way of Suffering. It portrayed the path Jesus was forced to traverse on his way to his crucifixion by Roman soldiers.

In those days, pilgrims were allowed to carry a light cross as they journeyed down the ancient path in order to imitate Jesus's journey. Much to my horror, people came out of their houses and from the shops that lined the streets, shouted epithets, and spat on us just as they did when our Lord carried His cross. All of us experienced shame and indignity, and we were shocked that people were behaving this way even today. It filled me with sadness. The tour guides took it all in stride, almost complacent to this act of betrayal that they witnessed every day.

Our trip continued, and we were graced with seeing the many beautiful and wonderful places where historical and biblical happenings occurred: where Jesus gave the people the beatitudes, the land of Canaan, where Jesus changed the water into wine, and the hillside where He multiplied the food. Every experience was deeply emotional. The tour guides were well-versed and gave many teachings along the way. I was particularly struck by one of the teachings. The guide explained that the shepherd we would see on the hillside never drives the sheep. Instead, he gently pushes them in the direction they should go. I pondered that the shepherd treats his sheep much like Jesus has treated me by always gently nudging me in the right direction.

Seeing the shepherds tenderly caring for their sheep reminded me of a story shared by another visitor to the Holy Lands. The bus filled with tourists was returning to the hotel when a woman sitting in the back of the bus became very agitated and called the tour guide to the window. "Come here! Look! Do you see that shepherd? He is driving the sheep. I thought you said that shepherds don't drive their sheep." Quite calmly, the guide responded, "Oh, ma'am, that isn't a shepherd. That is a butcher. He is taking the sheep for the slaughter."

That simple statement has remained with me all my life. The shepherd never drives the sheep; the butcher does. Reflecting on my life, I realize how true this has been. Jesus is a gentleman, He never demands, He just gently asks.

When I returned home, I realized God had unlocked a new way of thinking, and I viewed the world differently. We had seen extreme poverty in the Holy Land, and the counterpart was America's extreme commercialism.

The journey to understand how to blend the world we lived in with the desire to serve God was beginning. What does it mean to walk in Christian discipleship? Instead of looking back and reflecting upon every poor decision I had made in my life, I understood that God doesn't view us as foolish or disappointing but rather as treasures to His kingdom.

9

OUT OF THE DARKNESS AND INTO THE LIGHT

ONE OF THE MANY blessings that God gave us in Phoenix was the genuine friendship of Rosemary and Chano Traslavina. They taught us what it means to walk in discipleship.

As a couple, they were part of the Hispanic community our Phoenix friends ministered to in South Phoenix. My first introduction was to Chano, who was attending a conference where I was teaching. Chano was a gentle giant and quickly offered to help us set up. Little did I know that he had a very important role to play in my life.

You see for many months, I had an ongoing premonition of standing in front of a group teaching, and someone shot me with a gun. I prayed and asked for God's protection, but it was almost impossible to shake the foreboding feeling.

The first evening of the conference arrived, and we were all preparing for it to begin. As the room filled with people, I began to sense the Lord telling me to be very careful. We began as we always did with praise and worship. After about twenty minutes, an obviously disturbed young man entered through the side door and sat near Chano. Even from my vantage point, I could see that he was distressed. It seemed impossible for him to sit still. He would go in and out, unable to remain fixed in one place for very long. The Lord impressed on my heart to continue singing praise. People began to sing in the spirit. I felt God saying not to focus on the distraction. All we had to do was keep worshiping God.

Chano sensed the impending danger and approached the young man. He found him to be extremely agitated. We continued to sing, not fully understanding what was happening. Finally, I felt God confirm in my heart that we could begin the teaching. When I looked toward where Chano was seated, he was now alone.

Later in the evening, we learned that this young man had been taken to the emergency room. We were told that he was a veteran with PTSD, and that evening he was carrying a gun in his pocket with the express intention of killing someone. God arranged for Chano's capable assistance to intervene. Our God is awesome; He reigns from heaven above with power, wisdom, and love. Two weeks later, the man with the gun used it to kill himself. Thus, that intervention began our friendship with Chano, his wife Rosie, and their entire family.

We later learned that Chano and Rosie had been praying for weeks that someone would come into their lives to help them understand how to truly know God. Their prayer was for someone grounded in the Holy Scriptures to teach the truth. In their quest to learn more about God and their visits to various spiritual groups, they often felt that they were being wrongly informed. Our arrival in Phoenix was an answer to their prayer.

Rosie's Story: Our youngest daughter Connie was eight years old. She had been critically ill, requiring extensive hospitalization. The situation was beginning to look hopeless. The doctor told us it was time to inform our family because it did not look like Connie would live through the night. Our devastation was indescribable.

My brother had just returned from a mission experience, so when he heard of our family's plight, he said, "Why don't we all come together as a family and pray." Momentarily, my pride surfaced, and I thought, *What did he mean? Did he really think that I hadn't been praying?* Regardless, desperation for my daughter allowed me to put my wounded pride aside, and we gathered to pray in the room with Connie. Following my brother's direction, we began giving thanks to the Lord.

My heart ached as I gazed at my beautiful daughter lying in bed, her skin gray as ashes and her face covered by a huge oxygen mask. As we began praising and thanking Jesus, my little girl looked up, and without any prompting or informed knowledge, she began praising Jesus. I was shocked because this was not something that we had taught her. Instead of saying an eternal goodbye to our daughter that night, she began to get better. We had always attended church, but now I began an additional quest to take my little girl to any healing service or prayer meeting I heard about—it didn't matter what denomination. If they were seeking Jesus, we were there with Connie, and she continued to improve with each passing day.

While I was amazed and grateful for the healing that was taking place with Connie, I was irrationally filled with fear.

The fears that my grandmother and mother carried were passed onto me, and I took them on with a vengeance. My fear was beginning to paralyze me. My sleep patterns were irregular, and one day tired and filled with crippling distress, I heard as clear as a bell ringing from a bell tower, a man's voice saying, "Rosie, the demons are going to get you."

Those words sent my fear into an irrational overdrive. I began sending all my children to Christian counselors. We were all wearing rosaries around our necks. One day my brother said to me offhandedly, "You had better not tell a doctor what you are doing, or he might put you away." Our prayers for someone to come into our lives and help us now became loud shrieks to God.

Three weeks later, Franny came into our lives, and shortly after that, Chano was introduced to Marilyn.

They began teaching sound biblical principles, and while we were in our small group with them praising God, my fear would temporarily leave, only to come rushing back as soon as I returned home. My quest was relentless, and as we learned from the scriptures, something new was also showing up in my life. As I faithfully read my Bible, the words were revealing new understandings. I started slowly growing in my faith.

Although my fear subsided slightly, I had another emotion that dominated me when things did not go my way. I was filled with rage. The slightest imperfection would fill me with a reaction so forceful that anything in my way would be subject to my violence, and most of the time, Chano was the recipient of my uncontrolled outbursts.

The rage I carried was grounded in my earliest memories. My father was a disciplinarian. He desired to support his family, which meant that he worked long hours and was seldom home. He worked two jobs—a regular job during the week and on the weekend as a bartender and a bouncer, which didn't help his behavior. As a little girl longing for his attention, I missed him. When he was home, he would relax, and his relaxation would include too much alcohol. He was the family's overseer, and because of his childhood experiences, he had no understanding of how to handle his important parental role. He believed that heavy-handed discipline was the way to support his family. He was neither kind nor gentle. After I married Chano, he became the target of the rage I wanted to heap on the man who had disappointed me, my father, even though I felt love in my heart for him.

His actions toward me confirmed in my heart what I assumed to know—he did not love me. I longed for his love, yet every day, I was faced with my made-up, little girl's belief that I was not worthy to receive it. I still longed for it. My father's unrequited love led to fierce anger, and my unmet anger led to an enflamed rage. There was another element of this lonely existence that exacerbated my responses.

In the barrios, everyone knew everyone. A sister in one family would have five, six, or twelve other sisters or brothers, and they would have five or six children or more, which created tribes of families who I believed knew my family's dark secrets. I took on the personal responsibility of protecting my family name.

This only fueled more rage toward my father because as his daughter, I wanted and needed his protection. One day I went to the grocery store, and a boy from another family walked up to me with a large knife. He used it to stab me. Fortunately, I was holding a large loaf of bread, which saved me from possible death or severe injury. On another occasion, I knew my father was walking home from work with his friend Gilbert. I heard gunshots and thought someone might be shooting at my father. Without thinking, I ran to the kitchen door to go outside and protect him. I threw open the door, but it immediately slammed back in my face with the force of a gale. I learned later that my father's aggressors were lying in wait, and if I had gone outside, I would have been shot.

My family's secrets were numerous. One day while sitting around the kitchen table, my aunt said to me, "Why do you care about your family's name? You are not part of this family." I didn't understand what she meant, but once I heard her words, I felt an immediate rejection, which only added to my confused thoughts.

As the oldest, I was responsible for caring for my younger siblings. When my brother left, I was only fourteen years old, but his parting words were "You can have it all." This was the atmosphere I grew up in, and that atmosphere shaped my responses to life.

My rage was deeply embedded into every fiber of my being, but I could not express it then. Instead, I suffered from a myriad of illnesses. After the war, when I expected my father to return home, he instead traveled to California and enjoyed a carefree lifestyle for a while. When he finally returned to his family, my wrath was at a boiling point. Here I was, a little girl longing for my father's love, kissing his picture goodnight, holding it lovingly near my heart, and he didn't care enough to rush home to see me.

Anger was seething inside of me. I felt like a pressure cooker that was screaming for attention. The pressure cooker knob was violently shaking, and the heat was growing in intensity. My emotional immaturity and lack of familial support did not give me a framework to understand that I had a choice in dealing with my childhood traumas. Instead, I set in place a coping mechanism of rage that left nothing in its wake. The results of my rage would resemble an area that had been ravaged by an

F5 tornado—nothing was left standing. My illnesses as a child intensified. Sickness found a way to sideline me. I dealt with ongoing chronic illness year after year. Sickness and rage defined my life.

It was this rage that I brought into my marriage. My marriage to Chano was also filled with loss. Our second child Grace died three short days after her birth. Her diaphragm had not formed correctly in the womb; even after emergency surgery, our precious baby died. In addition to her internal health issues, she was born with a cleft palette. When the hospital's cleric came into my room to tell me that my child had died, he said, "I am not sure why God allows these monsters to be born." I was devastated and knew that whatever was wrong with my daughter was my fault. I was responsible, and that responsibility added more fuel to my unbending rage.

When our youngest daughter Connie was born, the doctor decided against caesarian surgery even though this meant I would have to deliver her breech. My baby came out bottom first, which resulted in substantial internal damage. I required a hysterectomy while still in my early twenties. I could no longer bear children, which saddened me greatly.

My marriage struggled. If Chano did something to upset me, it was not uncommon for me to throw whatever I was holding at him even if I was holding a knife. One day, I returned home from a hospital stay and thought Chano had been drinking. In a frenzy, I began scratching Chano's face. Reflecting on that moment, I realize I did not see Chano. All I could see was red rage. I had no control over my violent outbursts.

The next morning, I looked at my husband and was shocked. Chano had covered his many wounds with mercurochrome. The red treatment made the many scratches and tears scream for attention. Yet when I looked at him, I did not see Chano. I saw the face of Jesus, and I was deeply convicted of what I had done. I was forced to face the reality that my choices to deal with my emotional issues devastated my family and me. I had to find another way to deal with my open wounds. It was a staggering moment for me. This was the instant when I knew my behavior had to change. My deepest desire was to let go of my rage. In its place, I wanted to find peace but how? My aggressive behavior eclipsed the light of peace. When rage would settle over me, it reminded me of an eclipse of the sun. Darkness would cover me. How could the peace, light, and joy I desperately wanted emerge from such darkness? This was my battle.

Chano called Franny and Marilyn, and we gathered for healing prayer. I cried out to God in the most primal, primordial way I'd ever known. I cried for healing. I cried out for forgiveness.

The enemy was not willing to let me go easily. First Peter 5:8 (NIV) confirms that "the enemy, the devil prowls around like a roaring lion looking for someone to devour." He wanted to devour me, and my deep hurt and unloved heart and the sins of my ancestors had given him a cruel portal of access to me. Lamentations 5:7 (NIV), "Our ancestors sinned and are no more, and we bear their punishment."

I could hear the enemy's voice fighting for me, but in God's amazing mercy and goodness, I could also hear God calling me. God confirmed in my heart Romans 8:28, which states, "And we know that in all things God works for the good of those who love him, who have been called according to His purpose." I heard God's words, and I immediately felt something being lifted off me.

At that moment of total surrender, I was given spiritual insights. I could visually see a spiritual anointing in someone's life. I could also see when someone carried ill intent in their heart. I witnessed seductive emotions being negatively poured upon the opposite sex. If evil were present, I would smell a gust of sulfur. I rejoiced at God's anointing on my life although I needed time to understand what it meant and how to use these gifts effectively.

The rage did not leave me immediately. I spent long hours sorting it out with God and spent time in the scriptures. God brought conviction to my heart where it was needed. Everything Franny and Marilyn had taught us was confirmed through the scriptures. Our quest for knowledge was being rewarded.

I learned that God deals with everyone differently, not always how we believe He should or perhaps the way we would like. His way of dealing with me was to grace me with the opportunity to spend time with those who betrayed me although I am not sure I accepted it as grace at the time. Ultimately I was responsible for personally caring for three people from whom I experienced my greatest rejections—my father, my mother-in-law, and my aunt. All three needed help during the final years of their life.

I had secretly hoped my dad would pass before my mother because I was uncertain how I would communicate with my father without her presence. But here I was, my mother had passed on, and I no longer had her as the vital link between my father and me. She had been an anchor during many tumultuous years, and by default, I was now responsible for taking care of my father, the man who I felt did not love me. What was I going to do?

I tended to him for over two years, and over hundreds of cups of coffee that we drank together, I learned the deep wounds that my father carried. I began to understand his difficult life and how his childhood had left him with emotional deficits. My father could not give me what I longed for because it was not given to him. He quite literally did not know how. Through God's grace, I slowly began to respect my dad for his passionate desire to care for his family despite his many challenges. God in His goodness arranged for people to share stories of what my father had done for them during their life. These were important stories for me to learn, especially as my father and I were learning how to move beyond the pain that had been part of our relationship for so many years.

In his final days, as he was passing from this world into the next, I sat with him as a loving daughter, praying quietly by his bedside. We had learned how to communicate, albeit sometimes still clumsy, and I had forgiven him. Later in the evening, I walked outside, and as I returned to the house, I felt an amazing peace and calmness settle over me. I knew that he had passed, and the peacefulness I felt was his goodbye to me. When Chano came around the corner to tell me of my father's death, I acknowledged that I already knew. During our many coffee talks, my dad told me, "I wish I had been a better father." Forgiveness provided me with the opportunity to heal. I was now at peace.

Another hurtful relationship I had was with my mother-in-law. She was very unhappy that her son had married me, and her outspoken feelings reignited my latent feelings of rejection. When she became ill, I was once again called on to provide care. During my time with her, God revealed to me who she was and more importantly, why she behaved the way she did. While caring for her, I realized the wisdom she possessed, and I began to admire her. Forgiveness came naturally as a result of my love.

Another family member who had caused me excruciating pain was my aunt, and she too needed care in the closing years of her life. Once again, by God's mercy, I assumed responsibility during her final days. This time, God used the experience to show me some of my negative emotions and how my judgments of people were unjust to them and hurtful to me. Once I understood how my judgments of others negatively impacted my relationship with God, I worked to change my behaviors.

These experiences changed me, and God showed me how to *die to myself*. As a child, I lived every day just wanting to survive. Now I lived for God. With my newfound knowledge and love for God deeply rooted in my heart, I began to understand that only God knows what we need. He will not give us what we want, especially if giving us our wants will cause us to drift away from Him. God, in His infinite wisdom and mercy, will always lead us to Him, and sometimes as I learned all too well, the process can be painful. I had to give up all my woefully dependable coping mechanisms that had proven to be quite untrustworthy. I faced the reality of my need to truly forgive the many people who had hurt and rejected me. Occasionally the process was painful as I surrendered everything I had formerly counted on for my existence. I learned to embrace and welcome the discomfort. My once-eclipsed desire for God and His light was now present in my life.

I also began to realize something new that became profound learning for me. I was taught that my marriage to Chano was a spiritual covenant, a sacred agreement between God and us. I realized I had formed the habit of talking to everyone but Chano about my deepest thoughts, joys, and fears. My responsibility, as his wife, was to first discuss everything with him. A spiritual covenant was just that—a covenant. God required me to honor my husband. When I allowed others to know me more deeply than I allowed my husband, I committed a form of spiritual adultery.

As I continued to grow in my faith, God began showing me areas of my life that He wanted me to change. My journey was not without an intensely personal battle. I worked to give up my old attitude—a familiar attitude that once gave me comfort in its familiarity. Now when I resorted to an old behavior, I felt oppression come over me. This oppression took away my joy. Ultimately I realized I was responsible for coming face-to-face with my destructive behavior. Throughout my childhood, adolescence, and early married life, I had spent countless hours developing unacceptable coping mechanisms, which were deeply ingrained into my psyche. My behavior did not change overnight. With my heart fully open to God, He began working within me.

During this time of growth, I clung to God's Word, especially Romans 8:38–39 (NLT), which states, "And I am convinced that nothing can ever separate us from God's love." When those old familiar spirits would return to hassle me and convict me of my past behavior, I would claim God's precious Word over my life. I believed wholeheartedly that *nothing* would separate me from the love God had for me. This belief was my anchor.

I likened myself to an onion. As the old layers were being peeled away to reach the sweet core, the hard exterior skins of the onion peeled off quickly. The interior areas required more prayer and diligence on my part. As I constantly sought God, an overpowering sense of joy emerged.

Chano and I did not realize that at the beginning of our difficult journey, when we cried out for someone to teach us, God would gift us not only with prayerful teachers, Marilyn and Franny, but He would also give us a community where we could grow in the love of the Lord. I had no understanding at that time of how important it was to establish a community where we could be radically unguarded about every aspect of our lives, and we would never feel judged or condemned. It was a profound experience to be loved with Christian love. This experience opened the pathway for God's drastic healing not just for me and my husband but for our entire family, which consists of grandchildren and great-grandchildren today. Everyone has benefited and continues to benefit throughout all the generations. God wants His kingdom on earth to grow by cherishing our Christian brothers and sisters. That is community.

10

THE POWER OF
FORGIVENESS

AS FRANNY AND I journeyed through scriptures, individual and corporate prayer, and walking in discipleship with the body of Christ, wisdom increased. We were blessed to have witnessed God's healing power to others and sometimes to be used as instruments in their healing.

Franny and I spent evenings praying with many individuals seeking God. We quickly realized that the unforgiveness of past hurts and negative judgments could hinder healing for many. The pathway to healing would be opened if the prayer recipient was willing to acknowledge their previous behavior, ask forgiveness for themselves, and forgive others. We learned that forgiveness is the God-given elixir for healing.

Occasionally it would occur to me that although I was teaching suffering souls about forgiveness, I personally struggled with unforgiveness. One day, God presented me with a difficult teaching about my own inadequacies in forgiving. Our small group participated in a healing conference. We were eager attendees and wanted to soak up the many blessings we knew with faith would be available. Our hearts were open.

During the conference, I noticed a woman who was also attending. I knew a little of her history from past experiences with her, and I was aware that she had many difficulties in her life. This participant seemed to be front and center for every event. She wasn't part of the staff, but to others, it might seem that she had a leadership role. I tried my best to quell my feelings, but the more I saw her seeking attention, the more intense my internal spiritual struggle grew. Toward the end of the conference, Fr. George asked anyone who wanted prayer for the anointing of gifts to come forward. Franny and I quickly conferred, and we both desired to attend the conference to draw closer to God and receive personal healing. We were not seeking public prayer, so we sat quietly, praying contently in a beautiful, holy environment.

During my quiet personal prayer, I felt a tap on my shoulder, and a gentleman asked if he could pray over us because he and the woman, who had become my nemesis, didn't have anyone asking for prayer. I inwardly groaned. No! I did not want her to pray over me. I looked at her in utter disbelief. Franny, in her gentle way, agreed and the prayer began. The woman began speaking with great fervency over Franny, but it appeared to me that it was all for show. She was claiming words over my friend that made no sense. Franny began to weep. Every fiber of my being wanted to yell at her, "Stop. Get out of here!" Instead, they pushed me into the chair and simultaneously began praying about the healing of my leg. This woman went on and on, again with great fervor, claiming all her assumed medical knowledge. While every instinct in my body wanted to run, I could gently hear the Lord telling me to stay quiet. I argued with God and asked, "Why don't You boot her out?"

At this moment, I noticed a lovely woman I knew from our prayer group during our time in Tucson. She gently approached and said quietly to me, "Marilyn, God is asking you to forgive. He shows me you are of two minds, but you must choose forgiveness."

My heart was moved. In this tender moment, God revealed to me the importance of forgiveness and *His* deep love for this woman shouting prayers over me. I realized then that we all have resentments, unmet family needs, or painful experiences that we hang onto for reasons unknown or because they give us a false sense of power. I had come from a family that had immediate strong reactions toward things. We either liked someone, or we didn't. Yet at this moment, I knew regardless of my history or any built-in justifications to be right, I had a choice to make. My family's experiences, thoughts, and inward frustration did not matter to God. For total healing, God asks us to forgive and to forgive fully. I had a choice to make. I chose forgiveness.

Many years later, Franny attended a medical conference. At the close of the conference, she called me to say that another attendee didn't have a place to stay for the night. She asked if she could bring someone home, but she didn't want me to be upset. Of course, I agreed only later to discover that it was my former nemesis. God showed me the power of forgiveness. Giving true forgiveness allows God's blessings to flow. Our guests stayed for three nights, and we had a lovely time together.

I learned a lot about forgiveness through this experience. As it states in Romans 12:2 (GNBUK), "Do not conform yourselves to the standards of this world but let God transform you inwardly by a complete change of your mind. Then you will be able to know the will of God—what is good and is pleasing to Him and is perfect." Left to my device, I would not have forgiven. I allowed God to change my heart and to give up, allowing me to receive.

I have prayed with literally hundreds and hundreds of people of all ages and ethnicities over many years, and unforgiveness is usually at the heart of despair or an individual's lack of healing.

I am reminded of a story from an individual who has prayed with us over the years. He has a significant medical and spiritual ministry with cancer patients. He shared that when he is praying with a patient seeking healing, he asks them, "Is there someone that if they were present right now, you would feel uncomfortable?" The response is often yes. He then asks them to put their hand over their heart, envision the person standing in the room, and openly forgive them from the depths of their hearts. He has learned in his medical practice that forgiveness is one of the channels that opens the power of healing.

Forgiveness does not mean that if the person did something egregious to you, you condone it or say it is OK. The heartfelt statement of forgiveness means that as an act of will, you are choosing to forgive. It may take time for the emotions to catch up, but by repeatedly returning to God and reaffirming your forgiveness, eventually the emotions respond. Forgiveness returns your power.

Sometimes when a person comes for prayer, we would recognize that the spirit of oppression had been passed down from one age to the next. We would witness multigenerational families struggle with alcohol or drug abuse, divorce, thievery, or other negative patterns. Harmful and habitual behaviors would become engrained in an ancestral family line, wreaking havoc on unsuspecting descendants by creating lifetime strongholds. As stated in Exodus 34:6–7, "The Lord passed before him and proclaimed, 'The Lord, the Lord, a God merciful and gracious, slow to anger, and abounding in steadfast love and faithfulness, keeping steadfast love for thousands, forgiving iniquity and transgression and sin, but who will by no means clear the guilt, visiting the iniquity of the fathers on the children and the children's children, to the third and fourth generations.'"

Through prayer, God would help us understand the root cause of someone's difficulties. We were shown that the causes of pain or life struggles often began with past generations. When people ask for forgiveness and forgive those who wounded them, we would see countless blessings unfold in their lives. We believe in God's rich promise in Deuteronomy 7:9, which states, "Know therefore the Lord thy God, he is God, the faithful God, which keepeth covenant and mercy with them that love him and keep his commandments to a thousand generations."

Most people with whom we prayed came to us with an internal struggle. I understood this struggle as I, too, sought to completely surrender to God. I would be convicted of my behavior, which I would share with full transparency with our trusted group. I would receive their uncompromising support while simultaneously being held accountable. We became a living example of what it means to be the body of Christ.

God began strengthening the gift of knowledge within our group. I had experienced this gift during our formative learning years, but God was working in each of us individually as we sought God's wisdom to become more proficient at hearing His voice.

As Rosie experienced a great transformation in her life, she was now a willing and loving participant sharing in Chano's healing. Chano had also experienced the wounds of a broken and fractured family. In preparation for God to reach deep into the recesses of Chano's heart to heal him, He first prepared Rosie to love him tenderly and without judgment through the process.

We were learning what it means to serve with mature discipleship. We walked together in complete support of one another and began walking out. Philippians 4:6 (NIV) states, "Do not be anxious about anything, but in every situation, by prayer and petition, with thanksgiving, present your requests to God."

As I reflect on those years, one of the principal gifts I received was the friendship of Franny. She was a model of grace. Her constant prayer was for the Lord to give her patience, yet I would look at her and see only a loving and patient heart. Her devoted prayer life and her medical training enabled her to view everyone as an individual, and she never viewed anyone from a biased perspective. She taught me to look at people as multiple facets of a diamond, each sparkling uniquely. By viewing everyone this way, I was free to let God reveal what he wanted to reveal for them when we prayed—not what I thought someone might need. Sometimes we would start out praying for one thing, and the Holy Spirit would lead us down another path. God was able to show us the fundamental cause of our pain when our hearts were free of judgment.

On one occasion, we were praying with a gentleman in search of healing. He carried many fears and had an acute fright of water. In fact, unlike many young men, he hated going to the ocean. As we prayed, someone in the group asked, "Have you ever been buried?" The man gasped as a childhood memory came rushing back. He was playing with his young cousins by the side of a riverbank one day, and they decided to bury him in the sand in a mean-spirited way. Under the sand, his breathing was labored, with the sound of lapping water near what he feared was his burial site. He could also hear his cousins teasing him that the water was rising. This memory was buried in the deep recesses of his mind and long forgotten although the experience had unknowingly impacted many of his behaviors. It served as the root cause of the fear he carried. Through God's mercy, the memory was brought to the surface. The gentleman was able to process what happened to him and God, in His infinite mercy, healed him. The fear was released.

We learned the importance of what it means to serve with the Body of Christ. We were keenly aware that we did not want to do anything that would hurt the heart of God or grieve the Holy Spirit. The transparency we cultivated with our prayer partners provided accountability within the group. It was difficult for negative impulses to trip us up because of the answerability that existed within the group.

Work for the kingdom flourishes in a trusted community. Our enthusiasm to be used by God can also be exploited as a weapon by the enemy, who is always scouring the earth in search of souls to destroy (1 Peter 5:8). The wrong word or even the right word delivered without God's love may be hurtful.

There was something else that we began to realize. In addition to our nonjudgmental and trusted environment, we all deeply believed in God's providential care. Trusting Him daily and knowing that He would provide regardless of how bleak it looked amplified our steady growth in God.

In my childhood and early years, negative circumstances would cause me to react in anger based on fear. Now I rested in His abiding trust. I learned the meaning of Hebrews 12:11–13 (SJV), which says, "No discipline seems pleasant at the time, but painful. Later on, however, it produces a harvest of righteousness and peace for those who have been trained by it. Therefore, strengthen your feeble arms and weak knees. Make level paths for your feet so that the lame may not be disabled, but rather healed."

11

THE HOLY SPIRIT: OUR INTERCESSOR, COMFORTER, AND COUNSELOR

GOD SENT THE AMAZING Holy Spirit to help us all the days of our life. He promises in John 14:16 (NIV), "And I will ask the Father, and He will give you another Advocate, to be with you forever."

And what an advocate! When Jesus gave us His Spirit to be our intercessor, comforter, and counselor, He allowed us to grow in all areas of our lives with the presence of the Holy Spirit. The scriptures reveal a trove of magnificent crown jewels known as the gifts. These gifts are available to you and me.

I am often asked, "How do I receive the gifts of the Holy Spirit?" My answer is simple. Just ask. Our gracious and good God wants to bless you!

God's magnificent gifts have never been taken away from God's people. They were given to the first Christians and are still being given freely today. If you are inquiring how to receive these gifts, I celebrate you because it is an important question to ask. Why? Simply because when we seek and receive the wondrous gifts of the Holy Spirit, our lives benefit (Romans 11:29 ESV).

The challenge is that sometimes, we get sidetracked. Shiny new objects come along and capture our attention. Human nature's quest for new and shining attractions has changed our society and culture. The world's passion for God has weakened over the years, causing many people to drift away from our churches and ultimately, from God causing us to become lonelier and less productive.

Having prayed with many people seeking peace, comfort, and healing, we have often found that they have lost touch with God or have never had a personal relationship with Him. They have never met the real Jesus. Sometimes a shiny new object attempts to fulfill what a person thought was missing in their life. Through prayer, the Holy Spirit sometimes reveals hidden wounds. These wounds can emotionally paralyze the person and prevent complete healing. We also recognize when we pray with others, that holding onto our hurt can be a place of power. Unforgiveness can be as powerful as forgiveness because it serves our need to control. Forgiveness, on the other hand, can be completely liberating, healing, and comforting.

The Holy Spirit freely gives gifts, but to attain the fruit requires our commitment to walk consistently in Christian integrity, which is to fulfill the will of the Father in 1 Corinthians 12:11 (AMP), "All these things [the gifts, the achievements, the abilities, the empowering] are brought about by one and the same [Holy] Spirit, distributing to each one individually just as He chooses."

God expects us to ask for the blessings we need. Jesus taught in Matthew 7:7 (KJV), "Ask, and it shall be given you; seek, and ye shall find." However, God also says in Proverbs 15:29, "He hears the prayer of the righteous." When we sincerely strive to obey God's commandments and walk with integrity, He will give us answers to our prayers. He also knows if we are ready to receive answers. The heavens open when our heartfelt desire is to please and bring glory to the Father.

Earlier I wrote of my profound hurt and disappointment when we unexpectedly had to leave El Paso. Although I had searched my heart and felt God had called me to serve there, many years later, I understood that my personal agenda impacted my desires. I believed that because I would be working under a cleric, I could toss aside the leadership mantle that I sometimes found tedious. Through this painful experience, I learned that God never asks us to abandon our gifts, and because I chose my way, I was unhappy and made others unhappy too. More circumspection on my part would have given me improved discernment about my own humanity. I believe God called us to El Paso, but the unfortunate ending resulted from my doing, not God's. Often we get in the way of the plans God may have for us even when they might be quite stunning! In these critical times, it is important to understand how to grow in God's grace to combat a very active enemy who is attempting to tear down the kingdom of God. Even in God's Word, we are told in 1 Peter 5:8 (ESV), "Your opponent the devil is prowling like a roaring lion looking for someone to devour."

What is the answer for today's world? It is for us to continually seek the wisdom of the Holy Spirit. If you have been away from God, begin by first acknowledging your absence. Return to our gracious God with a simple prayer of repentance.[1] He is always

---

[1] A prayer of repentance: God, I am an unworthy sinner. I have sinned against You, and I come before You now asking for Your forgiveness. Please forgive me for (insert your personal sins). I acknowledge that by Your stripes, I am healed. Thank you.

listening, always. John 5:24 says (NIV), "Very truly I tell you, whoever hears my word and believes him who sent me has eternal life and will not be judged but has crossed over from death to life."

In the last chapter of Mark, Jesus commissions everyone, you and me included. Why would God teach us about His gifts unless He wanted to give them to us and for us to receive the fruits from them? In Galatians 5:22–23 (NIV), we are told, "But the Spirit produces love, joy, peace, patience, kindness, goodness, faithfulness, humility, and self-control."

If you have read this far, I believe you want all that God has to offer and more. Has a door been opened for you? Are you willing to help open a door for another? While writing this book, I have been reminded that my growth can be attributed partly to the Christian community. During the sixty-plus years of my walk with God, He changed the community as my needs changed.

Without the community, I don't think my development would have been as consistent and balanced. The experience of walking with other godly Christians committed to the Holy Scriptures steadied me through all the twists and turns of life. In community, I found accountability and intense trust. Never, and I repeat, never did I find judgment or condemnation from other community members even when sometimes my behavior may have been perceived as chaotic.

A Christian community is a profoundly deep experience where we show up to receive the love of God through others. There is another added benefit. A well-founded, seeking community adds order to the participants' lives. In the absence of order, there is chaos.

In our hunger, we need one another, and learning how to depend on each other helps us as we mature in our faith. God promised in Philippians 4:7 that He will give us peace, but just like everything else in life worth having, we have a role to play. Being part of a prayerful and loving community takes every participant's personal and committed effort.

I encourage, strongly suggest, and highly recommend that you consider forming or joining a Christian community. A loving community has the potential to reap huge benefits for your life. Committed participation provides the opportunity to turn the ordinary into the extraordinary! Like everything else though, it does require submission to godly principles.

As you continue reading, I claim these verses over your life, Psalm 128:1–4 (TPT): "How joyous are those who love the Lord and bow low before God, ready to obey him!" Yes, this is God's generous reward for those who love Him.

12

DISCIPLESHIP

THE GREATEST GIFT IN my life has been my personal relationship with Jesus and getting to know the Holy Spirit. This relationship opened the door to renewal in every area of my life, and it was the beginning of my understanding and living as Christ's disciple. Discipleship, as defined by *Merriam-Webster*, is "the condition or situation of being a disciple, a follower, or a student of some philosophy, especially a follower of Christ."

The New Testament provides a road map for the discipline of God's people. Life itself is the material from which our daily experiences become our spiritual school. It is here we begin to understand the wonderful gift of free will. God freely gives every person the freedom and opportunity to determine for themselves their response to life events. How do we respond, for good or for ill? The opportunity to choose occurs many times a day. It is precisely here that the Holy Spirit begins to write upon our hearts if we allow Him.

My decision for Christian discipleship began when I comprehended and sought forgiveness for the many things I knew were displeasing to God, especially in the area of friendship where my motivation was often selfish. I began to understand 1 Corinthians 12:31 (NIV), which speaks of "the way which surpasses all others, the excellence of the gift of love." As I studied this passage of the scripture, God's love and light began to shatter my heart with a completely new understanding of what His love could be. We must aspire to live the life God designed for us. He lived, and He died demonstrating incomprehensible love.

When I reflect on the days, months, and years that followed my life's surrender to God, I remember how timid I sometimes felt. In fact, I might say that I tested the waters with fear and trepidation. I knew that I did not want to return to any version of my former self. I wanted to discover all the realities of goodness that were previously unknown to me.

When I was first introduced to the Holy Spirit, I experienced an immediate quickening of the presence of God in my life. Something within me was awakened. My natural curiosity was to understand how to access these wonderful gifts and how I could be part of ensuring God's plan for my life. After several frustrating attempts to find a format, I began to understand that there was no formula for success with the Holy Spirit. As I studied the miracles and healings Jesus performed in the New Testament, I realized that each occurred uniquely and with freedom. *Jesus healed everyone who approached Him with belief.*

I approached God with heartfelt belief.

When someone would talk about the gifts of the Holy Spirit, I didn't know how He could give a gift or how I could receive it. Would this gift arrive at Christmas? I was in this new place with an aura of expectancy. People were praying and listening for the Lord. For a new and inexperienced person, it was strange. The first time I heard a prophetic word in our small prayer group, I felt an inner peace that I knew was from God while asking, "Is that really you, God?"

It took a while for my anxiety about the unknown to subside. One could say I was like Zacchaeus, the tax collector, who had heard about a man named Jesus. Zacchaeus was so curious about this man that he climbed up a tree just to get a glimpse of Him. After he met Him, he surrendered his life completely and joyfully even though he did not understand immediately. That was me. I was just like Zacchaeus. I was seeking God with all my heart. I would climb a tree or run out on the street if it would help me to get to know Him better. I didn't know how much He would reward me for persistently seeking Him.

During my journey with God, I learned that He sometimes teaches His people about obedience by presenting unusual opportunities. In my case, it was something so unusual that I felt utterly uncomfortable. This happened while ministering to a friend struggling with metastatic brain cancer. We had begun doing weekly prayer on Saturday morning called *soaking prayer*. This would allow a person to come each week and receive extended prayer with those prayer team members present. On this particular day, we gathered around my friend whose recent brain scans and X-rays revealed the gravity of her condition. As I began to pray, I was seated behind the reclining chair where she rested. Suddenly I began to feel God speaking firmly to me, asking me to stand up and shout at the brain tumor. My immediate and forceful reaction was to say, "That's not You, God. You would never ask anyone to do that." Regardless, the emphasis on my heart became stronger and stronger even though I argued unsuccessfully with the Holy Spirit for several minutes. I began to realize that this was something God expected me to do.

I did not like the request. I do not like shouting. In fact, I deplore shouting as a communication method, but at God's insistence, I finally stood up and announced what I felt I must do to everyone in the room. I placed my hand on the back of her head and shouted as best I could, "Cancer! Be gone in the name of Jesus!" Apparently, I had more to learn about obedience because God said, "Do it again." This time I was more obedient and responded without arguing. "Cancer! Be gone in the name of Jesus!"

The following week, the astonished physicians informed her that a new scan revealed that the tumor, which had been the size of an orange, was now gone! Did my shouting cause this remarkable healing? I don't think so, but it taught me something about obedience even when uncomfortable. Thankfully I have never been asked to shout again while praying with someone, but this experience was necessary for me to understand that God doesn't always explain Himself, and He doesn't do anything without it being good for our spiritual growth.

Seek discipleship with Jesus. Ask Him to be the light for your path. Claim the psalmist's words in Psalm 119:105, "Direct me, oh Lord, I will draw near to you. Thy Word is a lamp until my feet and a light unto my path." I remember my friend Patty telling me how much she yearned to know more about Jesus. One Sunday while sitting in church, she silently asked Him to open a path for her so she could know Him more intimately. While walking out of church that very day, a woman approached her and asked, "Would you like to join our Bible study?" When we say yes, Jesus has the most astounding way of making unexpected and miraculous things happen. Throughout my life when I needed someone or something, it would appear exactly when I needed it. Eventually as I matured in my Christian walk, God used me to show up for others seeking Him.

I have learned that we need one another.

If someone had told me at the beginning of my spiritual journey, "You need a community," I would not be sure if I understood what that meant. With the gift of time, I now recognize that the spiritual friendships God supplied for my journey have strengthened and fortified my path with God.

God placed me in three separate communities. My first community was in Tucson, followed by a community in El Paso, and later in Phoenix. Each experience was unique, and while I was unaware of it at the time, each group gave me the tools I needed at the moment for God's planning for my future. As Paul wrote in 1 Corinthians 13:11 (KJV), "When I was a child, I spoke like a child. I thought like a child, I reasoned like a child; when I became an adult, I ended my childish ways," I grew emotionally and spiritually with the help of those with whom I collectively shared my journey. I was being equipped and trained. I just didn't know it. Sometimes others would come and go, and although I didn't always understand it, I now see God was moving in everyone's lives.

What is a spiritual community?

It is a gathering place for those committed to growth in their Christian walk. Community is grounded in the purest form of love that Paul details in 1 Corinthians 13. A community comes together sharing the belief that Jesus Christ is the one and only Son of God, and they trust the authority of the Holy Word. The group's leader is the Holy Spirit.

Paul teaches us that we are the body of Christ, and as part of His body, we are responsible. More specifically, Paul commands a message of love. To the Church of Corinth, he says, "If I speak in the tongues of mortals and of angels but do not have love, I am a noisy gong or a clanging cymbal" (1 Corinthians 13:1 NRSV). What does that mean for you and me?

When misunderstandings occur, our responsibility is to address concerns at that moment. Never let a grumbling fox gain a foothold. As I matured as a Christian, I did not let words that I may have misunderstood fester, and I was open to hearing what others wanted to say to me. I learned to listen without taking offense. Eventually I realized that sometimes what may have been confusing to me or even caused me angst was God working in someone else's life. My responsibility was to keep my eyes focused on Christ. When I did that, all other irritations fell by the wayside.

In his book *The Art of Exceptional Living*, Jim Rohn writes about the early Church's founding and the response to one of the greatest sermons of all time, the Sermon on the Mount. He writes, "Some people who heard the sermon were perplexed. Others found it interesting. Some were amazed. Some who heard the sermon mocked, laughed, and made fun of the words spoken." He points out that there will always be mockers and grumblers, but those who heard the message and believed it ultimately changed the course of history. This example shows us the importance of leaving the grumbling and complaining behind and instead, striving through discipleship to be the loving Christian and change agents that our world desperately needs.

Community allows us to discover how to stand with one another using the scriptures as a roadmap. In a prayerful and trusting community, members become Christ to one another. There are no mockers or grumblers. The trust is so profound that everyone can openly share the details of their life, knowing that information will be received without judgment or condemnation. Consider Rosie and Chano's story. If the community had displayed any hint of judgment, would they have been able to willingly share in a manner that ultimately led to their complete healing?

There is something else that occurs when we grow in a community. We allow others to mentor us. Most importantly, we become mentors to others who may be seeking. I can unequivocally say that my friend Rosie is as much a mentor to me today as I was to her during our early years together.

Sounds impossible? Consider this.

When we are Christlike in our actions, our lives reflect discipleship. We bask in God's responding grace described in Luke 6:38, "Give, and it will be given to you. Good measure pressed down, shaken together, running over, will be put into your lap. For with the measure you use, it will be measured back to you."

13

SEEKING GOD

MY LIFE'S WORK HAS shown me that God truly desires to fulfill the destiny He has for all of His children. If we ask, the Holy Spirit will guide us exactly how we need to be guided. I became a seeker of knowledge. I attended conferences, read spiritual books, and sought God by studying the scriptures. I became intimately involved with Jesus through prayer. A solid prayer life is an important requisite to growth.

Simply stated, prayer opens heaven and allows God's blessings to reign down. Based on my years of spiritual mentoring many individuals, I believe that too few people fully understand the power of prayer. Prayer paves the way. Would a friendship deepen if we never or just occasionally talked to our friend? In the beginning, I talked to Jesus just as I would any friend, although I had to learn to manage distractions. That is exactly how I speak to Him today although our friendship is much deeper now. I discuss everything with Him. He has made it known to me that He is quite interested. He loves hearing the details of His children's lives.

There is a secret sauce to prayer. It is praise and thanksgiving. The late Derek Prince, a well-known evangelist during the twentieth century, is quoted as saying that if he only had ten minutes to pray, he would spend the first seven or eight minutes in praise.

There are 334 verses in the Bible about praise. One of my favorites is found in Psalm 100:4–5 (ESV), "Enter the gates with thanksgiving and His courts with praise! Give thanks to Him; bless His name! For the Lord is good; His steadfast love endures forever, and his faithfulness to all generations."

Faithful and authentic prayer results in miracles.

In chapter 4, I referenced one of the Holy Spirit's gifts, the gift of tongues. A dear friend of mine was ready to give up trying to receive this gift. After listening to a tape by the late Fr. John Hampsch, she decided to try a technique he recommended. She began singing, making up words she didn't understand to a familiar gospel song. She admitted to feeling a little awkward. While performing this exercise, a word came to her that she had never heard before, and it didn't make any sense. She chuckled to herself and thought that if she remembered the word the next day, it might mean something. The next day that word and a host of other words came to her. She was given the gift of tongues. If you have this gift, exercise it. The results are powerful when we approach the throne of mercy using the Holy Spirit's words. If you desire this gift, ask God for it. You, too, might consider singing strange words in your car with your favorite gospel hymn.

Along with prayer, my spiritual walk was simultaneously blessed with a love for the scriptures. I didn't have enough hours in the day to read God's Word. Sadly that is not always what I hear from others. Sometimes the scriptures are described as hard to understand or elusive. I know people who have struggled for two or three years, and suddenly, the words leap off the page. Even if it takes time, understanding the Word of God is a consummate gift from God. He is writing it on our hearts even if we are not aware of it. He wants us to apprehend the wonderful words He has written for us. Reading the Gospels while understanding the historical figures and experiences found in the Old Testament provides a deeper understanding of Jesus's walk on earth. Reading the Old and New Testaments faithfully presents a unique perspective. It is like seeing the skyline of a magnificent seaside city while instantaneously seeing the water on the shoreline.

In the early days of the charismatic renewal, gifted spiritual leaders traveled the country, teaching about the baptism of the Holy Spirit. I attended one of these events in August 1969, which jumpstarted my life. I am now at the stage of my life where I sit in awe at everything that has happened. I can't even remember all of God's blessings because there have been so many. I want to remember every single detail. God took an ordinary life and made it extraordinary. He can do this for you too.

I am thankful for the blessings, including the challenges I faced. Every challenge led me to a deeper, more intimate relationship with God. The almighty God brought order out of my chaotic life, which was caused by my own irrational demands and desires. He transformed my heart often in ways that I didn't know needed transformation. If you seek transformation today, He wants to do that for you too!

I will say that even at an age that many consider to be advanced, my bags aren't fully unpacked. I am happily aware that this marvelous adventure is not yet over. My heartfelt prayer for every reader is from the words from Psalm 37:4 (NKJV), "Delight yourself in the Lord, and He will give you the desires of your heart."

Over the years, I had an unstated desire to write a book. I wanted to share the astounding lessons with which God had gifted me. Many times I had received prophecies that indicated I should or would indeed document my life. When the thoughts could no longer remain tucked away in the back of my heart and mind, I was confounded by the fact that I had no understanding of what it would take or require from me. It was time to do what God had taught me to do, pray. At this final stage in my life, God has gifted me with a lovely group of women united in God's love and prayer. We call ourselves the Gracie Group. The name we have given ourselves represents many dimensions of our lives, but chief among them is God's beautiful grace in our journey together, that grace which called us together for these times to find God's path for love and service. I prayed with these special spiritual friends seeking direction and discernment as to how to start the process.

I knew that I could tell stories with great flourish, but I did not have the gift of writing. My good friend and a member of the Gracie Group, Pat Leach, suggested that I begin by identifying titles for ten chapters. She offered her help in organizing the information. She did not consider herself a writer and did not offer to do any writing. One day while driving along, she was thinking about the most effective way to organize the information, and she felt a nudging to begin writing. She said to God, "You know I am not a writer." In response, she sensed the Holy Spirit saying, "Start with the train story." She vaguely remembered an early story in Marilyn's life about meeting her mother on a train. Upon her return home, she called Marilyn and asked her to retell the story. A few hours later, the beginning of chapter 1 was completed, and we began the process of my sharing and her writing. The preceding pages are the result of her gifts and generosity.

Now a little more than a year since we began our adventure, I feel called to finish that work, a work that was sometimes exciting, heartwarming, and unbelievable, and occasionally I admit, there were moments where I was awash with tears of sorrow and joy. Yet throughout the process of sharing my experience of life with the Lord, He was always encouraging me, correcting me, guiding me, forgiving me, and sometimes needing to deliver me from my own mistakes or influences, which were not from Him. I close with the last chapter of this book with a story entitled "God's Mysterious Ways."

14

A FINAL STORY

AFTER YEARS AND YEARS of marvelous encounters with God, He is still surprising me. Let me tell you about the Delgado family who we met in El Paso and recently reconnected with. Now years later, we are ministering with the children of this family, and they continue to bring joy into our lives.

When we arrived in El Paso, Franny and I were assigned to *shepherd* some of the newcomers in the prayer community so they could begin to minister to others based on the Gospel message of Jesus. It was at this time that we were introduced to the Delgado family, which included the mother, Connie; her husband, who was affectionately nicknamed Cabuz (pronounced as caboose); and Connie's sisters, whom they welcomed at the time of their marriage due to the early death of their parents. This rambunctious family was delightful, and we took much joy in their friendship as we got to know them.

They all shared their love and care for one another. The youngest child Jesse was four years old when we met them, and I marveled at what appeared to be prophetic gifting. It was stunning to see some of the words he would speak that clearly were not his own but rather spoken with an authority that only could be God-given. With the benefit of twenty-twenty hindsight, perhaps God was preparing this family for something that only He could know was coming.

You see when we first met Connie's husband Cabuz, he was not pleased with the spiritual influences that were taking place in the family. He felt very strongly that he was the husband and father and outside influences were not invited or welcomed. We would have many late-night phone calls from Cabuz where he made it abundantly clear that he did not want the teachings of the Bible to be offered, and he was not going to permit his family to be involved, and that was that! Period!

I recall sitting at the top of our staircase many times listening to his scolding sometimes well into the night. He was adamant. The prayer group and anything connected to the work of the Lord were not to include his family. When he felt that he made himself emphatically clear, we would say good night, and I would often fall into bed not knowing whether I should laugh or cry with no understanding of where this was headed and how in the world God would handle this much animosity.

After a number of weeks of being on the receiving end of Cabuz's relentless diatribe, there was a strange episode at the Delgado home. One night an intruder broke in while they were sleeping. The thief awakened Cabuz and instructed him to pick up a pillowcase and follow him throughout the house, filling it with all the items he intended to steal. To make this additionally terrifying, he carried a large knife in one hand and threatened to kill him if he made a sound. The robber would point with the knife what he wanted as they quietly made their way through multiple rooms. As they entered the back of the house, there was a window approximately eight feet from the ground. Cabuz chose this moment to react. As he bent over to pick up an item that the robber wanted, he rose with the full strength of his weight expecting to push the robber through the window. The force of the hit was so hard that both of them hurled through the window, hitting the ground with a thundering might. Cabuz immediately got up to find that there was blood all over the small yard, some of which was on him, but the thief had vanished into the night. Cabuz hobbled to the front door and rang the doorbell to awaken his wife, who gratefully had slept through the entire ordeal. When she saw her husband, she was stunned and became very emotional. At this point, everyone was awake and shocked at what had happened. A trip to the emergency room revealed that Cabuz had a cut on his arm and a sprained wrist.

The experience stirred the dormant spiritual desires of Cabuz's life that he had up until now resisted so strenuously. Within days, he sought out a priest who prayed with him. Cabuz gave his heart and life to God, and his life was transformed!

Several nights later, Franny and I were teaching a class. I noted that Connie wasn't there, and I wondered if it was because of the family dynamics. Much to our surprise, when we were leaving, I saw Connie and a man walking toward us. I suggested to Franny that we say a quick prayer because I thought she was probably walking with Cabuz, and I had no idea what we were in for this time.

As he walked toward us, he asked, "Are you Fran and Marilyn?" When we acknowledged that we were, he reached out his hand and said with the greatest of kindness, "I am Connie's husband, and I want to say that both of you are welcome in our home any time day or night. I would be happy to see you."

At this point, we did not know about the event that occurred at his house, his miraculous transformation, and the work God had already accomplished in his life. The power of that moment when Cabuz welcomed us into his home was not lost on Franny and me. We were all overwhelmed with tears of happiness. We knew that God heard and responded to the many faithful prayers of family and friends, and He had performed a mysterious intervention while sending His protective angels. What followed was many spiritual fruits including Cabuz's involvement in the ministry. When we departed El Paso several years later, it was with tears and sadness that we left this wonderful family.

We have learned in our lives that sometimes the Holy Spirit leads us from one place to another. The beauty of the Christian family is that it always attracts others to come and share the good news thus community forms over and over and over again. This is how it was in the beginning with Jesus's first disciples. They left and spread the Gospel as He directed to the entire world. I like the expression I heard once which reflects my thoughts, "Bloom where you are planted, but don't get potted."

We kept up with the beloved Delgado family, but following the passing of both Connie and Cabuz a number of years ago, our communications with the younger generation had not been as often as we would have liked. Unexpectedly in the past couple of years, several of the siblings have renewed the relationship, and we are now exchanging frequent phone calls and phone ministry. Ernie, their second youngest son, and his wife now have adult children living in Phoenix so we have the joy of occasionally visiting with them face-to-face.

Here I am, many years later, still encountering people from the past while entertaining new people on God's highway. While I can't see or hear from everyone, I always keep them in my heart and prayers. One day I look forward to rejoicing together with Him and all whom we have loved on the road to eternal happiness.

The End
I Pray Blessings on Every Reader's Life

EPILOGUE

Dear Disciples of Jesus,

After many sessions of prayer ministry and study, I feel the need to communicate some of my thoughts regarding your status as a person of caregiving, nurturing, and loving as Jesus has called us to, i.e., a disciple.

We now live in a time which provides a wonderful window of opportunity to bring the healing love of the Savior to a very hurting, dangerous, and lost world. You have already ministered to those who could find no immediate help for health problems or emotional or spiritual crises, a circumstance in which you and your prayer partners became the source of help and healing. These needs were not able to be met simply by medical treatment or the good counsel of the Church; sometimes it was a financial inability, sometimes it was fear, and often it was discouragement; sometimes it was because the pain was so deep the person couldn't help themselves. But then, along came Jesus, and along came those wonderful instruments of sharing—the Macnutts, Schlemens, Evans, the Mullens, Sandfords, et al, plus many others too numerous to mention; Christians who had experienced the healing power of God in their own lives and felt a call to share it with everyone they possibly could—and somehow also, along came you. And, you wanted to bring comfort and healing and to make things better for others, so you said *yes* to Jesus, and *yes* to learning about prayer in a way perhaps you had not experienced before; perhaps sometimes you even felt a little uncomfortable in your role as a prayer minister, but you persevered and Jesus worked through that yes with which you responded and you began to see others respond to the power of the Holy Spirit as you loved and prayed. People were improved, or comforted, or given new understanding, or encouragement, and some were remarkably healed, and you were often surprised at your role as a minister of healing and sharing the love of Jesus with the brokenhearted.

The Lord has now placed in my heart a need to encourage you to pursue your gifts of caregiving and nurture, your gifts of loving and healing and blessing and not to grow weary in well doing. We have too long been too cautious in sharing Jesus. I believe in the days immediately ahead there will be times when medical help or perhaps the sacramental ministry of the Church will not be readily available, but we will always have access to Jesus, who is the ultimate healer, and we must not forget His gifts in time of trouble.

I remember well Franny's ministry in The Dump many years ago, and her comments to visitors who wanted to find antibiotics and other treatments to aid the illnesses of the people there. She would say "When we don't have access to medical care, we have the miracles of Jesus, and we must pray for them." And, pray they did, and miracles happened, and now so must we begin to understand more deeply the great power of the magnificent Lord who came to set us free from sin, sickness, and disease.

We do not know what lies ahead for our wonderful country, or what types of impediments to normal daily life may occur, but we do know that Jesus has come to walk with us through every eventuality. Difficult times are also great opportunities for the world to see the love of God in His people. We have been wonderfully blessed to know Him in one another and we have seen and experienced His power at work among us as He has healed the sick, performed miracles for which we have prayed, comforted the afflicted and sometimes *afflicted the comfortable*. We have seen His creative power in the brain of an infant, the healing of tumors and other cancerous lesions, the transformation of sinful lives into new life in Christ, and the homecoming of those who had wandered away. We have been given the best of all worlds, which is to live and participate in the Body of Christ and to share His love with one another.

I encourage you to find life in His Word and strength for the journey by participating fully and often in the sacraments, and in your spirit to "look up (to Jesus) for our salvation draws near," and particularly to rejoice in what we have been called to share in a ministry of comfort and prayer and love.

I am not expecting that we shall be blown away by terrorists today or tomorrow, rather I am expecting that whatever lies ahead, wherever we may be, that Jesus is both the answer and the provider for all our needs and that from His abundance we may always share with others, sometimes just an encouraging or comforting word, sometimes the laying on of hands with prayer for healing, sometimes leading a lost soul to the Lord of life when life is not certain, sometimes with our material possessions, and sometimes just to be present and steady when all around us others are hurting or afraid, or to be the touch of Jesus when a soul transitions from this world to eternity with Him.

Jesus has provided so many wonderful helps for us in today's world; we have access to wonderful physicians and care providers; we have the gift of Jesus available in daily Eucharist, and we have one another—I exhort you to *fill up* on the Word regularly, to take seriously the desire of Jesus to use you in a profoundly important ministry of healing and to become so in touch with the Holy Spirit that when you gently lay hands upon another, healing will begin. We can see that Jesus is not about bandaging wounds of the heart, but healing them, we shall experience healing of our own uncertainties, brokenness, and fear. As you look at your hands today, or at any time, know that they are truly extension of the hands of the Master and He wants to use them often to give His comfort, blessing, and healing. What an encouragement to know that in this city and many other places in the world, there are growing numbers of Christians who really desire to listen, love, and pray! We must join them in intercession and thanksgiving for the opportunity today to witness the love of Jesus in a suffering and frightened world.

God Bless You!

Marilyn

ABOUT THE AUTHOR

Marilyn Bodine is a recognized spiritual leader and teacher who, with assistance from her friend, Patricia Leach, began writing her first book, *Prayer Paves the Way*, at age ninety. She is pleased that after years of marvelous encounters, God is still surprising her.

Printed in the United States
by Baker & Taylor Publisher Services